DH 308 0101

D0214242

Northwest Historical Series
XVI

Dionisio Alcalá Galiano

Cayetano Valdés

Commanders of *Sutil* and *Mexicana* during the 1792 voyage.
Courtesy of Museo Naval, Madrid.

The Voyage of
Sutil and Mexicana
1792

The last Spanish exploration
of the northwest coast of America

Translated, and with an introduction by
JOHN KENDRICK

THE ARTHUR H. CLARK COMPANY
Spokane, Washington   1991

———

LIBRARY OF CONGRESS CATOLOG CARD NUMBER 90-52753
ISBN 0-87062-203-X

Library of Congress Cataloging-in-Publication Data

Espinosa y Tello, Josef, 1763-1815.
    [Relación del viage hecho por las goletas Sutil y Mexicana. English]
    The voyage of the Sutil and Mexicana, 1792 : the last Spanish exploration of the
Northwest Coast of America / translated, and with an introduction by John Kendrick.
    260 pp.   cm. — (Northwest historical series ; no. 16)
    Translation of: Relación del viage hecho por las goletas Sutil y Mexicana.
    ISBN 0-87062-203-X
    1. Northwest Coast of North America—Description and travel. 2. Northwest Coast
of North America—Discovery and exploration. 3. Indians of North America—Northwest
Coast of North America. 4. Malaspina, Allessandro, 1754-1809—Journeys—Northwest
Coast of North America. 5. Sutil (Ship) 6. Mexicana (Ship) 7. Spaniards—
Northwest Coast of North America—History—18th century. 8. Online.   I. Series.
F851.5.V68   1990
917.9504′2—dc20   90-52753
                                                           CIP

Dedicated to
KAYE LAMB
with respect and affection.

CONTENTS

ILLUSTRATIONS

MAPS

ACKNOWLEDGMENTS

The author gratefully acknowledges the advice and assistance of Dr. Donald Cutter at an early stage of this work, and his valuable comments on the manuscript when it was finished. Dr. Janet Fireman provided a check list of documents in the Archivo General in Mexico when the author was starting his research. In Vancouver, Mercedes Fernández Durán solved some puzzles in interpreting several obscure passages, although she bears no responsibility for any errors that remain. In Mexico, Dr. Manuel Miño Grijalva and Dr. Mario Real de Azúa made their research available to the author. In Madrid, Director Juan González Navarrete of the Museo de América gave permission to include copies of drawings from the Bauzá collection in this book, and also showed their collection of northwest Coast artifacts to the author, while Concepción García Sáiz procured the photographs. Also in Madrid, Almirante Director Vicente Buyo Couto of the Museo Naval gave his generous support and granted permission for publication of drawings and maps from the museum, while his research team of Dolores Higueras Rodriguez, Maria Luisa Martin-Merás, and Pilar San Pío Aladrén provided the cheerful and generous help known to all researchers at the Museo Naval.

Part One
Introduction

INTRODUCTION

THE NORTHWEST COAST

History, it has been said, is not what happened, it is what has been written. So it is with the voyage of *Sutil* and *Mexicana*, two small ships which left Acapulco in March 1792, to explore the waters inside the Strait of Juan de Fuca. That voyage, as recounted by the explorers themselves, is the subject of this book. Their objective was to settle the question of whether there was a passage leading from the Strait of Juan de Fuca to the Atlantic by way of Hudson Bay. As it turned out, this was the last of the many Spanish voyages of exploration of the west coast of North America north of Cape Flattery, voyages that had all been undertaken during the preceding eighteen years. During that time, the outer coast had been explored as far as the Russian outposts in the Aleutian Islands, as well as some of the fjords leading inland. The last of these prior voyages, in 1791, had been an attempt to find a way to the Atlantic via the mythical Strait of Anian. It was commanded by Alejandro Malaspina, and he it was who inaugurated the voyage of *Sutil* and *Mexicana*.

Malaspina had left Cádiz in 1789, on a voyage that was to have taken him around the world. He had two corvettes, built expressly for the voyage. They were *Descubierta* and *Atrevida*, the latter under the command of José Bustamante. During the eighteenth century, exploration of the Pacific had been intensive, with English, French, and Dutch explorers taking part. Spain, after a century of exploration in the South Pacific ending with the voyage of Quirós in 1606, had made no further significant discoveries in that area. In the face of all the activity by other nations, Spain decided on a Pacific odyssey of its own. When Malaspina came forward with a proposal for a voyage around the world, it was accepted. By that time, the broad outlines of Pacific geography were known, and Malaspina proposed a "politico-scientific" voyage, which would include scientists of many disciplines, and the best hydrographers in the Spanish service. One of these, fast becoming pre-eminent, was twenty-nine-year-old Dionisio Alcalá Galiano.

Malaspina reached Acapulco at the end of 1790. Before that time, Malaspina had decided that he would forego the glory of another circumnavigation, and spend his time on more detailed scientific studies and surveys in South America—extensions of those he had already carried out, both on the coast and during extensive forays into the interior by his scientists. At Acapulco, Malaspina waited for Bustamante, who had taken *Atrevida* to San Blas. There Bustamante received orders from Spain, which he transmitted to Malaspina when he got back to Acapulco. The orders required him to divert from his planned itinerary and go north along the American coast to sixty degrees latitude to find the Strait of Anian, which was supposed to lead to the Atlantic Ocean. These orders resulted, as did the voyage of *Sutil* and *Mexicana*, from a paper written by the French geographer Phillipe Buache, whose reputation did not depend on the reliability of his maps. He had revived the story of one Ferrer Maldonado, who said he had sailed to the Pacific Ocean from the North Atlantic in 1588, emerging from the Strait of Anian in sixty degrees latitude.

Royal orders must be obeyed, so whatever his private thoughts may have been, Malaspina set off for Alaska, a voyage which cost him the better part of a year, and a planned visit to the Hawaiian Islands. He detached Galiano from the expedition and left him in Mexico to bring into order the mass of astronomical and geodetic information gathered in South America, and to carry out other investigations in Mexico. Malaspina did not discover a route to the Atlantic, but he did gather some geographical and ethnological information which fitted in with the purposes of his voyage. On the way back he called in at the Spanish outpost at Nootka, which had been set up in 1790 after a preliminary visit by Esteban Martínez in 1789, and was under the command of Francisco de Eliza. Malaspina learned of explorations of the Strait of Juan de Fuca made during 1790 and further explorations which were under way. This strait was the site of another mythical passage to the Atlantic, but had not been explored to its end by Eliza and his officers.

In 1790, Manuel Quimper had explored the Strait of Juan de Fuca as far as the present San Juan Islands that screen off the eastern end of the strait. His map showed several bays on both sides of the strait, but he could not see what lay beyond the San Juans. In 1791, Eliza himself took his ship as far as the Puerto de Quadra, which Quimper had discovered and mapped. He sent the small schooner *Santa Saturnina*, which had accompanied him as consort, through the San Juans to explore the present Strait of Georgia. Its commander, José María Narváez, reached and named Cape Lazo at the northern end of the Strait of Georgia, and roughly mapped both coastlines. On the eastern shore, he showed two islands with a large river running out past them, and the appearance of a wide inlet reaching inland. He was looking at the estuary of the Fraser River, but from offshore could not see the low lying land between his two apparent islands. The journal of Narváez, if he wrote one, has been lost; all we have is Eliza's report on the eight day reconnaissance by Narváez. In that report, Eliza said that if there was a passage to the Atlantic, it must lie through the opening behind the "islands."

Malaspina had no time to spare for an exploration of Juan de Fuca, so he returned to Acapulco. He refitted his ships there and set off on his voyage across the Pacific. He got as far as

Sydney, then returned to South America for more studies, arriving back in Cádiz in 1794. That voyage does not concern us, but before he left Acapulco, he made an intervention with the Viceroy that led to the voyage of *Sutil* and *Mexicana*.

THE GALIANO VOYAGE

When Malaspina got back to Acapulco from Alaska in 1791, he learned that Madrid had also heard of the explorations of the Strait of Juan de Fuca, and that the Viceroy of New Spain, the Count of Revillagigedo, had been instructed to send another expedition to Juan de Fuca and explore it thoroughly during 1792.

Revillagigedo had assigned a recently constructed ship named *Mexicana* to this task, under the command of Francisco Mourelle, one of the officers from the Department of San Blas, the naval base on the Mexican west coast. Malaspina proposed that rather than sending Mourelle, some officers of his own expedition should be detached and provided with the necessary chronometers and instruments, and that two ships should be used, *Mexicana* and *Sutil*, which latter had followed *Mexicana* off the ways at the shipyard at San Blas, but had not yet been out of the harbour. He proposed that Galiano should command the expedition, and that Cayetano Valdés should command the second ship. As seconds in command, he proposed Secundino Salamanca and Juan Vernacci.[1] Revillagigedo accepted this, and Malaspina's candidates, all of whom had been officers in his ships, were appointed. A draftsman cum artist named José Cardero was also detached. Cardero had started out as a member of the crew in *Descubierta* and succeeded one of the artists of the expedition who was disembarked at Lima. Ten members of the crews of the corvettes also volunteered to join the northern voyage.

---

[1] The spelling of Vernacci's name is taken from his signature on various documents in the Museo Naval in Madrid, hereinafter cited as "MN." His name was variously spelled in other documents, including the narrative of the voyage.

Malaspina issued his instructions to Galiano and Valdés, then departed on his explorations. Revillagigedo did not leave it at that, but sent a letter to Galiano with his own instructions for the voyage. These two sets of instructions are in conflict in some respects. Malaspina, not for the first time, suggested that collaboration, rather than command, was the way to conduct a voyage of scientific discovery, addressing this admonition to both Galiano and Valdés. The two sets of instructions, with covering letters, are given in translation in Part Two of this work.[2] These instructions were not available to Wagner when he wrote his *Spanish Explorations of the Strait of Juan de Fuca*. To understand parts of the narrative, a reading of these instructions is almost a prerequisite. There is a marked difference in style. Malaspina gives a call to glory, then suggests how he might do things if he were there. Revillagigedo just commands. Apart from style, there are some substantive differences. Malaspina does not even mention the possibility of a passage connecting to the Atlantic Ocean, which was the objective of the voyage in the view of the Spanish government. Revillagigedo treats it as more of a possibility, although he was doubtful about it. He gives instructions on advising him of what may happen, and on procedures to be followed on the voyage to Europe in the event that a connection to the Atlantic is found.

Malaspina goes into detail on a survey of the coast south of Acapulco, and the transfer of longitude calculations to the Caribbean and thence to Cádiz so that maps might be assembled from many sources. Revillagigedo just says that on their return to San Blas, he will give them instructions about the southern survey. The survey was not made, so presumably Revillagigedo cancelled it, or else Galiano decided against it and got the Viceroy to agree.

[2] Most of the information in the preceding paragraphs is well known, so references are not given. The instructions from Revillagigedo are in MN MS 619. There is another copy in Mexico, in the Archivo General de la Nación, cited henceforth as "AGN," in Marina 82, folio 204 et seq. Those from Malaspina are in the AGN, in Marina 82, folio 193 et seq.

It is not necessary to summarize the voyage here, but some collateral accounts should be mentioned. *The Voyage of George Vancouver* gives his version of his meetings with Galiano, and the journal of Juan Francisco de la Bodega y Quadra (See Bibliography) mentions the two visits to Nootka by Galiano's ships. There is a collection of miscellaneous notes covering a small part of the voyage, in MN MS 330, to be discussed later. In the present work, these accounts have been used as references.

Although the primary purpose of this work is to present the narrative of the voyage, many readers will share the author's desire to learn something of the individuals who set off in those inadequate ships to sail—and to row—through uncharted waters. A brief account of their careers is given in the Dramatis Personae which follows text.

Galiano ended his voyage in San Blas. The officers, plus Cardero, went to Mexico, where the Viceroy set them to work to prepare the narrative and the maps. Soon after the work started, Valdés, Salamanca, and Cardero left the city,[3] while Galiano and Vernacci stayed until the work was finished. They then returned to Spain, where it was intended that a full account of the Malaspina voyage and all its scientific findings would be published. This would include Galiano's exploration of the Strait of Juan de Fuca.

PUBLICATION OF THE NARRATIVE

When Malaspina returned to Spain, he gathered about him a group of his former officers to prepare the publication that was to eclipse the work of Cook or Lapérouse. Among these officers were Galiano and Vernacci. Galiano arrived back in Spain a month after Malaspina's return; Vernacci had arrived earlier.

Malaspina had enough free time to get into political trouble. There are several stories as to how this came about, but evi-

---

[3] Archivo Histórico Nacional, Madrid, Estado 4290. Cited hereinafter as "AHN."

dently he clashed with Manuel Godoy, the first minister, who had been given the title "Prince of the Peace." That clash was the end for Malaspina. He was confined to the fortress in La Coruña until 1803, then exiled to his native Parma, where he died in 1810.

The arrest was made on November 25, 1795, and the next day an order was issued impounding all the papers and ordering the officers back to their Departments.[4] Two of the officers named were Galiano and Vernacci. Galiano was working on his maps, and had prepared an abbreviated version of the narrative of his voyage for inclusion in the vast work recording the Malaspina explorations and studies. Reference will be made later to a partial manuscript of this narrative, which has been shortened and edited in Galiano's handwriting, with some additional corrections by Malaspina.[5]

Galiano obtained an exemption from the order, but his papers were impounded.[6] He was assigned to prepare a new topographical map of Spain,[7] but went back to sea in September 1796. This ended his connection with the 1792 voyage, since he was at sea in command of various ships until his death at Trafalgar in 1805.

The acclaim given to the publication of George Vancouver's narrative of his voyage of 1791 to 1795 may have stimulated the Spanish authorities to publish something of their own. The Malaspina voyage would have been an obvious choice, but Malaspina was still confined in La Coruña, and his name was not even to be mentioned. It was decided to publish the narrative of the voyage of *Sutil* and *Mexicana*. As far as the Malaspina expedition is concerned, this voyage was only a side trip for some of the officers, made on orders from Madrid. As far as the exploration of the Northwest Coast of America is concerned,

---

[4] MN MS 2296.

[5] MN, MS 1060. The author is indebted to Dr. Donald Cutter for drawing his attention to this manuscript, and for his identification of the handwriting.

[6] MN MS 2296.   [7] MN MS 2201

there were more significant voyages, notably those of Bruno Hezeta and Bodega y Quadra in 1775, of Ignacio Arteaga and Bodega y Quadra in 1779, and of Esteban Martínez and Gonzalo López de Haro in 1788. The choice of the 1792 voyage may well have been a matter of expediency. The manuscript was already in Madrid, and it was necessary only to edit it to remove references to Malaspina, substituting for his name "the commandant of the corvettes," or simply "the corvettes."

The narrative, with accompanying maps, was published in 1802, under the title *Relación del Viage* (sic) *hecho por las Goletas Sutil y Mexicana en el año de 1792 para Reconocer el Estrecho de Fuca*. It is cited hereinafter as *Viage*. It was republished in Madrid in 1958. The original edition was translated into English in 1911 by G.F. Barwick. Although his translation was never published it exists in typescript, and part of it was included in Wagner, 1933. Another translation was made by Cecil Jane in 1930, which unfortunately was published in that year. Unfortunately, because it is far inferior to Barwick's translation. The author has seen still another undated and uncatalogued English translation in the Vancouver Public Library, inferior to both of the above.

With all this material available, there must be strong reasons to justify the present work. There are some inconsistencies in the *Viage*, such as the inclusion of negotiations between Bodega y Quadra and Vancouver at Nootka, which took place after Galiano had left that harbour, and there are extensive quotations from Venegas, 1757. Another inconsistency is that the anonymous narrator appeared to be now aboard *Sutil* and now aboard *Mexicana*. There are differences between the published version and various manuscript copies of the voyage narrative, which in turn vary one from another. These are not serious matters in themselves, but suggested to this author that some further research might be productive.

The *Viage* was published without the name of an author. It

has been ascribed to José Espinosa y Tello, who had joined the
Malaspina expedition in Acapulco in 1791, in time to make the
voyage to Alaska. Espinosa was not aboard *Sutil* or *Mexicana*,
nor was he one of the officers working with Malaspina at the
time of his arrest.[8] The impounded papers were delivered to
Espinosa in his capacity as Director of the Depósito Hidro-
gráfico. Espinosa is not now thought to have been responsible
for the editing, an opinion this author has not been able to
confirm or refute. However, what was done is more important
than who did it. The evidence on the latter point is in the Museo
Naval in Madrid, in the papers in MS 1060 which have been
mentioned above. Espinosa could not have been the original
author, because most of the writing was done either en route or
in Mexico, at a time when he was voyaging with Malaspina.
Espinosa could not have seen any of the documents until he
returned to Spain at the end of Malaspina's voyage. As to the
identity of the author, more will be said later.

All of the documents contained in MS 1060 are incomplete
and undated. Nevertheless, there is enough material to trace the
course of the manuscript from the time when Galiano was
working on it in Madrid until it was published. The documents, numbered by the present author, are:

1.   The narrative of the voyage from Nootka to San Blas,
stopping at Monterey en route. To this has been added an
account of the Indians of Monterey. much of it taken from
Venegas, 1757. It has been extensively edited in Galiano's
handwriting, including the striking out of lengthy passages.
One page is missing, being misfiled in MS 2040. There are
some minor corrections in Malaspina's handwriting.[9]

2.   An account of the negotiations between Bodega y Quadra
and Vancouver, followed by a description of native life at
Nootka, the latter with an acknowledgement to José Mariano
Moziño, a naturalist from Mexico who spent six months at

---

[8] MN MS 2290.

[9] This document, in its original form, is the subject of a forthcoming book by Donald Cutter.

Nootka with Eliza. Document 2 has been amended and shortened in a different handwriting to Galiano's. As amended it corresponds fairly closely with the published *Viage*.

3. A fair copy of Document 1, as corrected. It is further amended in the same handwriting as in Document 2. With small differences, the amended version corresponds with the published *Viage*.

4. A one folio account of the voyage from Cape Scott to Nootka, with minor amendments which make it almost identical to the published *Viage*.

5. A description of Monterey, duplicated in Document 1 before amendment.

Study of these documents has led the author to the conclusion that the *Viage*, published in 1802, contains distortions that invalidate parts of it as an authentic account of the voyage. The evidence is not as complete as would be desirable, so the conclusion is based on a balance of probabilities. Document 1, with the handwriting of both Galiano and Malaspina on it, surely must have been amended during the time Galiano was working with Malaspina in Madrid prior to the latter's arrest in 1795. Document 3 is obviously of a later date, and since the amendments bring the wording very close to that in the published version, it is likely that it was amended when the manuscript was being prepared for the 1802 publication, after Galiano had gone back to sea. Document 2 supports this opinion, and includes the changes made to Moziño's *Noticias de Nutka*.

The other documents are less important, but do not contradict the above analysis. The doubtful points are:

1. The documents include only a part of the *Viage*; there is no evidence as to what happened to the rest of the narrative.

2. Since Galiano himself introduced some of the changes, it is possible that he found errors in earlier drafts.

3. The source of the alterations is not known, other than Galiano's abbreviation of his journal. This raises the possi-

bility that the changes might have come from an equally authentic source, now lost, such as a journal by Valdés.

There is no answer to the first point. As to the second, it would only be valid if the changes introduced by Galiano were inconsistent with the original on which he was working. In fact, he just abbreviated the original, and inserted bridging passages to maintain continuity.

With respect to the third point, it is clear that some of the changes are based on the then popular philosophy of Rousseau. The popularity of the theory that man in a state of nature is noble and pure did not extend to explorers. This theory is criticized in the journal of the voyage, in a passage deleted from the *Viage*. The only other voyage narrative of any length known to exist is the *Miscellaneous Notes* in MN MS 330 which describe native customs, as well as a brief account of the voyage from Nootka as far as Lángara. A pencilled note on the cover page of these notes, folio 56, states that they were written by Secundino Salamanca. This is based on a comparison of the handwriting with that in an entry by Salamanca in the Atrevida guard book.[10] This author does not find the comparison convincing, and the notes will be referred to as "MS 330." In places, Galiano's narrative is identical with MS 330, and in all likelihood those parts of the narrative were copied from it.

The reliability of the MS 330 notes is open to question. In writing of Apenas, daughter of the chief Macuina at Nootka, the writer states that she was married to a chief named Anikius. This is most unlikely. Moziño, who spent six months studying the Indians at Nootka in 1792, describes attending her puberty rites, which were followed by a ten month period of seclusion, a custom that has been reported by a number of later ethnologists. Galiano's narrative is taken from Moziño at this point. The editor of the *Viage* did not follow the MS 330 version of this event, and stayed with the account reported by Galiano.

---

[10] MS 755.

The extensive discourse in the preceding paragraphs is included because the present work in some measure replaces one that has been used as the primary source of the history of the voyage of *Sutil* and *Mexicana* since 1802; it seems necessary to give the reasons for this, and at the same time to describe other sources.

The importance of the discrepancies between the published work and an authentic account is a matter for debate. It is always preferable to have a first hand historical record than one which has been changed by someone who was not there, but apart from that, the ethnological material in the 1802 publication is in part invalid. This criticism applies especially to some of Moziño's writings, which have been altered and added to the publication. In places the published work contradicts what Moziño wrote, even though the editor said he was indebted to Moziño for the material. Moziño's account is available either in Spanish[11] or in English in the Wilson Engstrand translation.[12]

The Definitive Text

Having concluded that the *Viage* is an inaccurate account of the voyage, the next stage of the analysis is to select a definitive text. This is not to say that it is necessarily a true account. Galiano made some mistakes, as footnoted in the text which follows. He also exaggerated, particularly in his reports of friendly relations with the Indian people. His account of the discussions with Vancouver does not correspond with Vancouver's narrative, so one of them misunderstood or did not tell the truth. This is true of many historical events more important than Galiano's voyage.

There are many copies of the narrative of the voyage; some are abbreviated extracts, some are variants, and the incomplete texts in MN MS 1060 were edited and partly written in

---

[11] Moziño, published 1913.   [12] Wilson, 1970.

Madrid. It is necessary to identify one of the many copies of the Galiano narrative which can be considered to be definitive.

Galiano worked on the maps and narrative in Mexico from soon after his return to San Blas at the end of November 1792 until October 1793. He did not enjoy the confidence of the Viceroy, Revillagigedo. Revillagigedo was critical of Galiano's work, and he had to rework much of it, mostly to improve his rough writing style and to reconcile the place names in his journal with those on his maps. Finally, during the night of October 18th, 1793, either Galiano or Vernacci delivered the documents to Revillagigedo's house. Revillagigedo probably did not see the documents before Galiano and Vernacci left on October 20th, a Sunday, for Veracruz, to catch a ship for Spain. Revillagigedo wrote to Galiano at Veracruz[13] in the usual effusive style, to tell him that he had corrected a number of errors in the narrative, and had added some names which had been omitted from the maps. Among the omitted names, as he pointed out to Galiano, were the Island of Bonilla, and the inlets and islands of Güemes and Pacheco. Since Bonilla was the head of the secretariat, and Güemes and Pacheco were two of the numerous names of the Viceroy, this does not show too much tact on the part of Galiano.

In Veracruz, Galiano could not know the nature or extent of the changes made by Revillagigedo, so he wrote back urging him to send to the General Council of the navy in Madrid the original which he had deposited during the night hours.[14] Revillagigedo did not do this, but instead sent his amended copy to the Minister of State, including with it a list of errata, showing the changes he had made.[15] He also sent a copy of everything to the Navy Minister, Antonio Valdés. With the aid of the erratum list, it is possible to determine which manuscript is the one Galiano wanted sent to his superiors as the definitive

---

[13] Translated in Appendix 1, Letter B.   [14] Appendix 1, Letter C.
[15] AHN, Estado 4290. Copies in AGN Marina 92.

account of the voyage. A manuscript in the Museo Naval, under the number MS 619, is identical with the copy sent by Revillagigedo minus the changes. It could be the one sent to Antonio Valdés by Revillagigedo. It is signed by Galiano and dated in Mexico on October 18, 1793, the same date as the night-time delivery to the Viceroy's house. There are copies in which Galiano's name and the date have been copied as well as the text, which vary to some extent from MN MS 619. One of these is in the AGN in Mexico, under the number Historia 558. This volume includes the manifests of the ships, mentioned in but missing from MS 619, which are translated in Appendix 2. Historia 558 has also been useful in reading some obscured or obliterated words in MS 619. The wording in Document 1 in MS 1060, before the changes made by Galiano and Malaspina, is closely similar to MS 619, but includes other matter, such as the Venegas ethnography of California, which had been published in Madrid in 1757.

The erratum list is the key document. It includes 70 numbered items, for each of which the page number and the line number are given. Many of these are circled or underlined in MS 619, although this could be the work of some later researcher or official. Throughout, the line numbers quoted in the erratum list are identical with those in MS 619. The pagination is different. In MS 619 the text is preceded by seven folios, recto verso, of instructions. The text starts on folio 8, numbered folio 1 in the erratum list. The difference of seven in the folio numbering is maintained part way through, to the middle of Chapter V, where the difference drops to four. Later, in Chapter X, the difference increases by one, to become five. There is no chapter ending or other break in the text at the places where the pagination changes.

The pagination changes are unexplained. It is as if there were three blank numbered folios when the Viceroy's people edited Chapter V, and the same number was used twice in numbering

Chapter X. These postulates do not appear to be a likely explanation of the difference in pagination part way through the document. Other reasons could be advanced, but there is no evidence to support any of them. Despite this difficulty, MS 619 is regarded as definitive. The original wording, given in the erratum list, is identical with MS 619, and in a hand written document it is hardly possible that the line numbering would be identical between one version and another.

The erratum list has been useful in working out some puzzling sections of the text. Some of these sections also puzzled members of the Viceregal staff, who proposed likely interpretations in the erratum list. In one case, the Viceroy's scholars erred, not recognizing the word "estanco" (watertight, that is to say in seaworthy condition), correcting it to "estando" (being), and advising its omission.

Although Galiano did not know the nature or extent of the corrections made by the Viceroy or his staff, they are in fact inconsequential, mostly being spelling and grammatical errors, which for the purposes of a student of history are not of importance. The main purpose of the research described above was to identify a manuscript that could be confirmed as definitive. Having done that, this manuscript is a natural choice for the translation of the voyage narrative.

Galiano's signature on MS 619 does not prove that he wrote it. There is some evidence that he did not write all of it. There are some changes of format and style between chapters, which could be because they were written by different people, or because they were written at different times. The former is suggested by the identity between parts of the MS 330 notes and the journal, as mentioned. Also, there are passages in Chapter XII, footnoted where they appear in this book, referring to the Indians at Mulgrave, where Malaspina had anchored in 1791. These passages appear to refer to the narrator's own experiences. Since Galiano was not at Mulgrave, it is probable that he did not write this part of the narrative. There are references in Chapter IX of the *Viage* to the tides in the Strait of Magellan. The Malaspina voyage did not go through this strait, but Galiano had done extensive surveys there in 1785-6. These references do not appear in MS 619, and may have been added by Galiano while he was working on the documents in Madrid.[16]

The Museo Naval has numerous fragments of text. MS 2456 contains sketches that were made en route by boat parties. There are notes written on or accompanying some of the sketches. They add nothing to the narrative, but contain some material that has been copied into it. MS 144 consists of a number of partial drafts, heavily corrected, some of which are evidently copies by a scribe, and others probably written by one or another of the voyagers. Scrutiny of these does not indicate material which could have been the source of any significant portion of the passages which appear in the *Viage* but not in MS 619.

It is evident that Galiano used notes written by other officers or by Cardero in compiling parts of the narrative. Still, it is the author's opinion that he wrote most of it; the narrator always appears to have been aboard *Sutil*, although the first person singular is never used. In a number of places "we" is used to refer to the expedition or its members, in others "the goletas" or "they" is used. Where individual endeavours are described, the surname is used. All of the officers are named at some point in the narrative, but the artist Cardero is not mentioned other than in the manifest. This poses the question of whether Cardero could have been the author. For example, in Chapter IX, Valdés is credited with making a drawing which surely was drawn by Cardero, and is titled in his distinctive script. Still, it is this writer's view that Cardero could not have been the principal author. The narrator was familiar with navigation and seamanship, and with scientific, philosophical, and political matters

---

[16] The surviving part of the documents in MS 1060 does not include this passage.

that would have been beyond the grasp of young Cardero. In addition, the narrator is placed aboard *Sutil* at all times, while Cardero was a member of the crew of *Mexicana*.

THE TRANSLATION

Translators may often start with the intention of producing an exact duplicate of a document. For this work, such an intention collapsed with the first sentence of the narrative, which contains one hundred and eighty five words, of which the verb is the ninety fourth. Long sentences, and long paragraphs, have been broken up when this does not alter the sense of a passage. Stylistic changes cannot be avoided when this is done, but as far as possible the flavour of the original has been preserved. For this reason, the somewhat wearying superlatives scattered through the narrative have been retained, even where they are patent exaggerations.

The meanings of nautical terms in Spanish, which are sometimes different to meanings in general non-maritime use, have been taken from the 1831 Diccionario Marítimo Español. The Diccionario gives not only usage current at the time, but older meanings and older equivalent words of the same meaning. In translating, if there is a familiar English nautical equivalent it has been used, but where this equivalent is not apt to be understood by many readers it has been explained or paraphrased. For other Spanish words the primary reference was the Diccionario Enciclopédico Larousse.

Spelling of the names of people and places varies within the manuscript and accents are omitted. A likely or an authoritative standard has been chosen. Place names capitalized in the manuscript have been left untranslated, i.e. "Puerto de Nutca" rather than "Harbour of Nutca" or "Nutca Harbour." Where the designation is general, and is not capitalized, it has been translated, i.e. "la entrada de Fuca" appears as "the entrance of

Fuca," but Entrada de Ezeta is left unchanged. Present day equivalents for the places named in the narrative are given in the Glossary of Place Names, which follows the text.

Sutil and *Mexicana* were always described as "goletas." The word "goleta" has not been translated. Literally, a goleta is a schooner, but the term was used to describe a small seagoing ship regardless of rig. *Sutil* was rigged as a brig, while *Mexicana* started out as a topsail schooner, then was changed to a brig with an extra fore and aft sail on the foremast. It was accordingly considered inappropriate to use the word "schooner."

To avoid ambiguity, some English words have been inserted by the translator, enclosed in brackets thus: "To give the maximum capacity, the two bread lockers [with] which [the ships] came were made into one and waterproofed." Similarly, a few inserted dates, and words required because a sentence has been broken up, are bracketed. To restore the syntax of long sentences that have been broken up, minor emendations have been made. These are not bracketed.

In the Museo Naval manuscript 619, there are a few apparent copying errors, and a few more probable ones, which have been corrected and footnoted. A more serious deficiency exists in Chapter XVIII, where figures for latitude and longitude are inconsistent and some are obviously wrong. These have been footnoted but not corrected. In the same chapter, the toponymy of the Santa Barbara Channel Islands is obscure. This too has been footnoted.

The Museo Naval manuscript presents almost no paleographic problems. It is signed by Galiano, but is not in his handwriting. Where words are obscured, they can in most cases be found in the Archivo General manuscript (Hist. 558), or occasionally in the *Viage* published in 1802. The orthography in the manuscript is variable and sometimes unusual, which led to some translation problems, as did the search for syntactical antecedents that might be a page back. To save the reader a similar search, nouns have been used instead of their pronouns where necessary.

The voyage of *Sutil* and *Mexicana* was acclaimed by the Viceroy of New Spain, even though he criticized the orthography of the narrative. After two hundred years, the acclamation remains.

Part Two
Voyage Instructions

VOYAGE INSTRUCTIONS

1. INSTRUCTIONS FROM ALEJANDRO MALASPINA

Señores D. Dionisio Galiano and D. Cayetano Valdés:-

A new field of glory lies before you in the next commission of the Goletas Sutil and Mexicana of the Department of San Blas, and when the accompanying circumstances are considered, either in the service of the Nation and of all Europe in an objective which enters so deeply into the advancement of its knowledge and its navigation, or as the executor of the orders of the King and the stipulations of the Señor Viceroy, in a course surrounded by such thorns and perils, it will not appear strange that I assure you that I look with envy on the new path that you must tread out very soon.

You are not unaware that although the sayings of antiquity and the natural unity of command always give the preference to one [person], and while this will be true on every occasion on which the lack of time, the clarity of the objective, or the disparity of ideas does not permit a prior amicable agreement, nevertheless these occasions have been so rare in the corvettes Descubierta and Atrevida that it would not be temerity on my part to assure you with my infinite satisfaction that the way of these ships will be better effected by the friendly judgement of all the officers than by my limited directions at each instant of its short duration. Thus, neither have I for a moment doubted we both make common cause on these notes, nor will I ever doubt that on the present commission, on whatever is demanded by the good of the Service you combine the quality of friends and companions with the exact good order required by the same Service.

His Excellency the Viceroy of Mexico, as you will see by the attached copies of the correspondence[1] graciously agreed with my offer that two goletas from San Blas, under your orders, should sail next summer for the hydrographic and political discovery of the internal channels of the Strait of Fuca. I know that it is indispensable to add in each [vessel] another intelligent officer. I have named with this intent Frigate Lieutenants Don Juan Bernaci [sic, for Vernacci] and Don Secundino Salamanca. His Excellency only required, with attention to a just equality, that by this Ship Lieutenant Don Jacinto Caamaño and Frigate Lieutenant Don Francisco Mourelle both of the Department of San Blas, should not be considered excluded, they having formerly been entrusted with the command of the goletas. His Excellency also accepted that [the goletas] should go to Acapulco to complete their fitting out in this harbour and sail directly from here to the NW coast. He wished finally that the necessary conclusion of our tasks on the coast of Guatemala should be combined with this commission. I would systematize these notes relative to everything that may best tie the different objectives together, not omitting to inform you, as already I have suggested to His Excellency, that these notes which I now include for you are written, not because it is my spirit to restrict even remotely your steps, to which you will no doubt direct a rare zeal and intelligence, only to present to you one by one the different objectives which must be embraced so that our objectives shall be unanimous in favour of the good service of His Majesty.

1st   The principal and almost the only objective of your commission (entirely subordinated to His Excellency) is that of exploring all the internal channels of the strait of Fuca, giving

---

[1] Not translated or included in this work.

priority to the maximum penetration of the sea or navigable rivers towards the east to decide once and for all the excessively confused and complicated questions of the communication or proximity of the Pacific Ocean and the Atlantic in this parallel [of latitude]. Afterwards, a secondary objective is to look into the veracity of the words of the English Captain Meares in relation to the discoveries of the Lady Wasington [sic] and the Princesa Real and finally to ascertain for the true utility of Geography what are the true limits of the continent and how far to the east the archipelago extends, which so far has been explored between 48° and 56° of latitude.

2nd   In this exploration, all those practices which have been followed in the corvettes ought to accompany these instructions as secondary (let us say it thus), limited nevertheless to the fair extent that they are unquestionably preferable [in spite of] your small number, your multiple tasks, and the constriction and inconvenience of the ships. Thus, geodetic tasks and the political examination with reference always to national prosperity are excepted, both important matters. All the other objectives of botany, zoology, and lithology you will regard as fortunate accessories which cost neither the slightest risk or sacrifice of your own safety, nor the slightest loss of time on the part of the commission.

3rd   In all these objectives, it is useless for me to manifest to you the importance of following either the methods adopted in the corvettes for the division of matters, or other methods better and clearer. The necessary return to Europe of all elements before the publication requires that many officers must work at the same time, and this will not be easy if matters are not subdivided greatly beforehand.

4th   Having examined the smallness of the ships, the length of the voyage from here to the coast and the great depth of the internal channels of Fuca I have come to believe that before undertaking the exploration in mind, you should make a brief stop at Nutca, there replacing, with the help of the ships and establishment the stores and water consumed [on the voyage], replacing any sick, supplying yourselves with a good quantity of pine beer and thus making the succeeding explorations independent of any necessities and of dealings with the natives.

5th   I would not undertake the navigation of the Strait of Juan de Fuca before the middle of April nor in consequence the departure from Acapulco before the middle of February, and bearing in mind the proposed stopover at Nutca neither would I take on board as large a quantity of food as can be carried. It is better to reduce the quantity of water to a two month supply, and once inside the strait, without delaying at any point already explored, not even in the Boca de Quimper or that called by Captain Meares Rio Orenage[2] I would endeavour to attain the limits of the explorations of Ship Lieutenant Don Francisco Eliza to be able to continue new explorations, directing myself whenever possible towards the east. If this route should oblige me to turn towards the west until approaching the Canales de Princesa Real or the vicinity of the Islas de Bucareli, finding the sea in known longitudes I would turn back, and by another interior route set out in search of the mouth of the Orenage. Finally, cut off also in this part by the continental shore, I would try, if the season was still opportune, to approach, by the western shores, as close as possible to the Nuchimases.

6th   I have indicated to His Excellency the Viceroy that it would now be appropriate to substitute for the method thus far followed of taking possession for the Crown of Castile according to the formalities of the Laws of the Indias, the less equivocal and more universal method of an exact hydrographic determination, and of one coin or another buried in a bottle in which the day, month, and year of discovery is stated, and the vessels which have made it, adding to this precaution that of

---

[2] Meares shows the "River Oregon" flowing into the southeast part of Juan de Fuca, clearly meant to be the Columbia River.

buying from the natives with the greatest possible solemnity one or another of the places which appear most appropriate for a mercantile establishment, secure, healthy, and with a sheltered harbour, with easy communication with the sea, and an abundant trade in peltries, with fertile wooded soil suitable for seeding. I believe that our rights will be much less exposed to continual disputes with rival European Powers, and for us this would be of real and true advantage.

7th   I firmly believe that if in the event some strange and difficult circumstance does not intervene to prevent you, in no case should the goletas remain in the straits of Fuca beyond the middle of September. Also it appears to me that in case the interior explorations are completed sooner, navigation of the Canal de Reyna Carlota should not be omitted, and along the northern shores of Fuca, whose inlets from Cabo Frondoso are placed and arranged in much different directions on the English charts of Captains Dixon and Meares.

8th   I presume in consequence that it would be in the middle of September that you depart from these shores. The best method of tying together your explorations and ours will be to continue the coastal voyage, examining the accuracy of Captain Meares, which I believe somewhat suspect, and above all not omitting the examination of the entry of Ezeta, whose depth of only 25 fathoms at the entrance makes me believe that it does not extend far inland. A good harbour in these latitudes would be a most useful discovery for the fur trade and for the National interest.

9th   The harbour of San Francisco is a most important harbour for the California domains, and the corvettes, under the necessity of making a stopover in Monterey, could not explore it. It would be convenient and useful if your arrival for the required rest and supply of provisions could be at the former harbour rather than at Monterey. An excursion to the neighbouring missions, particularly Santa Clara, would provide you at the same time an agreeable respite, and to the nation that knowledge which at present is slight.

10th Since on the return of the corvettes from the northern coast it was their objective to arrive as soon as possible at San Blas and Acapulco, it was necessary to omit the exploration of the Canal de Santa Bárbara and the Islas de Santa Catalina and Santa Bárbara, of the Puerto de San Diego, and of the coast from that point to the Isla de Cerros. It would be useful to visit and to trace in detail these places, but this has to be with sufficient economy of time, sacrificing the least useful to the necessity that the goletas should be completely refitted in Acapulco so that they can leave by the middle or end of December to continue their voyage towards the coast of Guatemala.

11th Our explorations to the southeast of Acapulco have been recorded on a map of the small part situated in the vicinity of Aguatulco and the limit of our work continued from the south to the volcanoes of Guatemala. The exact definition of the intervening coast, and particularly the examination of the Puerto de Ventosa immediately on the coast of Tecoantepeque [sic] are now new objectives you must assume, although you should add next to those already indicated an exploration of the further coasts of Guatemala and particularly the Golfo de Amapala and the Golfo de Nicoya. It appears that for the better acceleration of the work and for making the best use of the opportune time, the goletas should separate, one working from Acapulco to the Barra de Ystapa, and the other from this place by the harbours of the Intendencia de S. Salvador to the Golfo de Papagayo and Golfo de Nicoya.

12th You well know how important it is to the uniformity of work in one or another part of America that the operations should be repeated of carrying to the other sea by means of the marine clocks the longitudes derived from our series of observations made in the various harbours we have visited. These operations already indicated before could very well be repeated in the entrance of Guazahualcos and at Veracruz, basing the first on the Puerto de Tehuantepeque, [sic] and the second either on the same Guazahualcos by means of a coastal voyage, or by land from the Capital already tied to the observations at Acapulco with an opportune observation of the first satellite of Jupiter made at dawn on the 29th of last November. The commission of one of the goletas would be concluded in consequence at the Barra de Ystapa, which should not expose to the slightest risk the primary objective of perfecting the hydrographic description of the coasts. It will be a work of little time to return to the Ventosa, and from there to cross to the other sea, making use of the coastal vessels directly to Veracruz, if circumstances permit, this being preferable to going directly to Mexico by road.

13th   It is clear that the indicated commission should not need instruments other than the sextant and the most reliable of the two pocket clocks presently assigned to the goletas. The complete collection of other instruments should therefore be delivered, either to the other goleta or to the Royal Captain General of Guatemala so that they can be sent on, and last (if His Excellency the Viceroy is in accord) return the ship belonging to Ventosa to its department. The assigned officers should undertake their return voyage to Europe, with the agreeable duty of presenting personally to His Majesty the fruits of the latest expedition and undertaking the placing in order of the various elements of the work.

14th   Many reasons of equity and of a just sharing of work, command, and responsibility lead me to believe that among you are those who should be directed with anticipation to . . .[3] and leave to Frigate Lieutenants Don Juan Vernacci and Don Secundino Salamanca the care of the tasks which include outside the Golfos de Amapala, Papagayo, and Nicoya, and inside (on the return of the goleta to San Blas from Realejo) a hydrographic map of the Golfo de Nicaragua and Rio de San ?Juan

---

[3] In the manuscript, some words at the ends of lines have been truncated in the binding. This particularly affects articles 14 and 15.

made with exactitude, so that neither the system of defense nor of trade should lack those data without which the successful provisions for the prosperity and security of that region would be very exposed.

15th   The ultimate reunion at the Barra de Ystapa, or whatever others . . . not distant from Guatemala, will be in consequence correct if the . . . of officers in the indicated plan has not been made beforehand in San Blas or Acapulco, or else if from one or other of these harbours you do not find it preferable to go directly to Mexico to avoid the straggling or delay of one of the goletas; leaving to Vernacci all the work on the coast except the transfer of longitudes to the other sea.

16th   It is not necessary to caution you (since I ought to assume it) again that the combination of these last tasks cannot be decided until the return from the Estrecho de Fuca, with attention to the dispositions of the Viceroy according to the circumstances which occur at the time.

17th   It is equally unnecessary to caution you that either the copy or the original documents of all the work of the first campaign should be sheltered from all risk of loss, causing them to go to Spain as soon as possible, the edited work and the notebooks and data going in two different ships.

18th   The draftsman José Cardero should remain with you embarked in the goleta under the command of Don Cayetano Valdés, Cardero having until now worked on the expedition with such assuredness and accuracy. His present monthly salary of 20 pesos should be continued for the account of His Majesty, or could even be increased to the amount that you propose and His Excellency the Viceroy approves on the condition that he must continue working for your commission in whatever work is prescribed for him.

19th   Accounting and reconciliation by the method thus far followed in the Descubierta is in all truth a burden at the same time onerous and tiring, much more so when the help of two excellent accountants is lacking, which is available in the corvettes. By paying attention to the sacrifices to the Royal Treasury which another method would entail, to the delays which result to the expedition, and to the disputes which are habitually produced, I earnestly ask you not to depart from the same method, avoiding any prolixity of documents for anything which is easy to form later in a report, but noting in a current book all the costs incurred and giving with them receipts corresponding to those amounts which are spent for whatever purpose in the objects of the Royal service. In this case, His Excellency having determined the benefits [due to] each of you, and anticipating according to the estimates the necessary funds, will have the kindness to give to you in this commission as well as in the succeeding one to the realm of Guatemala all that liberty to which the corvettes essentially have owed the celerity and good fortune that has attended them until now.

20th   You will receive these instructions from the hands of His Excellency the Viceroy to whom, as the necessary judge of all our doings and special protector of the commissions of the corvettes, I have submitted that he should soon affirm the instructions, to the greatest advantages of the Royal Service and to that good order and uniformity which are the base of success.

21st   You must not neglect to advise us in duplicate at Santiago de Chile and at Buenos Aires of the happy termination of your hardships nor forget for even an instant to take care with the greatest tenacity of your own health and that of all your subordinates, which care I can unhesitatingly recommend to you earnestly as much in the name of His Majesty and the Nation as in that of all those worthy companions who have admired until now your constancy and intelligence.

Our Lord grant to you many years.

Alexandro Malaspina

Corvette Descubierta, 6th of December, 1791.
Sres. Don Dionisio Galiano and Don Cayetano Valdés,

commanders of the goletas Mexicana and Sutil
of the Royal Navy.

This copy Mexico, 27th of December, 1791

[Signature] Bonilla.

2. LETTER OF FEBRUARY 7TH FROM REVILLAGIGEDO TO GALIANO AND VALDÉS, ENCLOSING INSTRUCTIONS

Although on the 27th of December last I sent to you the instruction drawn up with my agreement by Ship Captain Don Alexandro Malaspina, for the exploration of Fuca, Tehuantepec, and the Gulf of Nicaragua, I believe it to be desirable to issue another instruction relative to the first objective, which is that it must be completed promptly from the said Fuca to San Francisco.

I transmit it to you so that the operations of the voyage will be governed by its twenty articles, since besides its including very necessary advice in case an exit to the Atlantic by Hudson and Baffin Bays is found and for all the other events of the campaign it is also a reference, regarding the physical examinations, to the [instruction] extended with my approval by Don Alexandro Malaspina which must be observed and complied with in all the points not expressed here.

In the 3rd article I anticipate my orders to the Commandant at Nuca, that he should furnish the help available to him. [Since] Ship Captain Don Juan de la Bodega y Quadra now should be going to the same destination I give him the same responsibility, to the end that he should provide people, arms, boats, and whatever you request for the best performance of your duties.

Meetings with foreign ships or establishments being possible, I include for you the attached passport which will serve as credentials for use in such cases.

Meanwhile, if anything worthy of consideration occurs and which requires me to take steps, make it known to me since I will contribute everything to your success and the splendid completion of these duties of the service.

May God grant you many years.
Mexico 7th February, 1792
>[Signature] El Conde de Revillagigedo

3.   INSTRUCTIONS FROM VICEROY REVILLAGIGEDO

Instruction to be observed by Frigate Captains Don Dionisio Alcalá Galiano and Don Cayetano Valdés in the exploration to which they have been assigned of the Strait of Juan de Fuca, situated between latitude 48° and 49° North on the northwest coast of the Southern Sea.

1st   The principal objective of this commission is the complete exploration of the Strait of Juan de Fuca, giving preference to its northern and eastern limits over the details of its interior shores, without thereby omitting the execution of whatever should be possible in this part, making plans of its harbours, bays and islands, tracing the direction of its shores and whatever could lead to having an exact knowledge of this interior part of the globe, but without forgetting that what is most essential is the determination of the northern and eastern limits of the said Strait.

2nd   The two goletas assigned for this commission are to leave the Puerto de Acapulco when their commanders believe from their maritime knowledge that the time is opportune, selecting if they can that time which will bring them off the mouth of the said Strait in the middle of May.

This strait, and whatever others are found exiting to the Southern Sea,[4] are to be located as accurately as possible, both in latitude and longitude either with the marine clocks, by lunar

---

[4] The Pacific Ocean

observations, or by the satellites of Jupiter, but endeavouring to economize the time for these observations, it being sufficient that the results shall have the degree of confidence necessary for navigation, even though not having the scrupulous accuracy needed for astronomy.

3rd   Considering that the said goletas are incapable of carrying the necessary food and supplies for this extensive campaign, they are to proceed from the port of Acapulco to that of Nuca, in which their commanders will find whatever they need for the continuation of their voyage, remaining in this port only to refit the ships and regulate the rate of the clocks,[5] in the expectation that the commandants of that establishment will have orders to supply men, arms, boats, and whatever is asked of them for the two goletas to continue their campaign.

4th   Although it would be very helpful to explore the coast between Nuca and Fuca, the heads of this exploration should only undertake this if favourable weather permits it in passing, without causing the slightest delay, since that which is most important is to arrive early at the entrance of Fuca.

5th   As soon as the goletas enter it, they will determine its position exactly, and continue their explorations in the way they have been described.

6th   If the results of this inspection disclose any communication with the Atlantic by way of the Bays of Hudson, Baffin, et cetera, its entrance shall be fixed in the utmost detail, and the commanders of the goletas will set their course from it to Europe if permitted by the situation and their food supply, trying [to avoid] by every means touching at any foreign port, but in case they are obliged to do so through necessity, they will endeavour by every imaginable means [to ensure] that their place of departure and duties shall not be known, or at any rate the location of the connection that has been found.

7th   In this case, from the first European port at which the

---

[5] That is, the rate at which the clocks gain or lose time.

goletas arrive their commanders will give a secret despatch to Their Honours the Ministers of State and of the Navy, as well as to me, with a statement of the part of the coast that they were unable to explore, in order that coming to His Majesty's notice through these channels he can determine what I shall do further in his Royal pleasure, but if, the connection with the Atlantic having been effectively found, it is judged advisable not to proceed to Europe because of a scarcity of provisions, or because the ships are not suitable, they will be directed to Monterey if it is for want of provisions, and if because of the ships, to San Blas, their commanders giving me a secret despatch and explaining to me whatever they believe will lead to undertaking the campaign afresh to make a passage to Spain by the Strait.

8th If, as is probable, there is no such connection, the one to the Southern Sea[6] treated by the English voyager Meares shall be sought, and from this they will proceed south by the route inside the Islas de la Reyna Carlota, and attempting to explore the Archipelago de Princesa Real, of which Meares also spoke.[7]

9th A clarification will be attempted as to whether there is a connection between this part and Fuca, and the goletas having navigated it inside, continuing the examination of the shores of the Strait, endeavouring to get clear of it by the end of August, or by early September, to continue in that month and October a detailed exploration from Fuca to San Francisco, sailing into the Boca de Ezeta as far as supplies and the time permit, determining the true position of the Rio de Martín de Aguilar,[8] and entering ultimately the port of San Francisco.

10th If no connection is found to the Strait by Princesa Real or elsewhere, the goletas will sail offshore, and in such a

---

[6] The Pacific Ocean

[7] This paragraph refers to a map Meares included in the narrative of his voyage, which showed a reported sea whose western shore runs northwest from the Strait of Juan de Fuca and returns to the Pacific north of the Queen Charlotte Islands. Such a sea does not exist, but there are narrow passages inside the offlying islands for most of the distance between these latitudes.

[8] This is a river reported by the survivors of the Aguilar voyage in 1602. Its identity has never been established.

case they can determine the coast accurately between the Strait
and Nootka. Even if that connection is found, the goletas will
sail offshore if the commandants find this necessary for some
reason. In this way they will be able to refit in the Puerto de
Nuca, since even if that establishment is then delivered to the
English, I will advise those responsible for the delivery in
advance in order that they should agree with the English that
they will assist those ships if they arrive at their harbour in need,
or provided that they are advised that it is found impossible at
the time to sail, or with urgent need of repairs.

11th   Once that which has been referred to up to this point
has been carried out, the principal part of the commission of the
goletas is concluded, in compliance with His Majesty's orders
which he has communicated to me through His Excellency the
Count of Floridablanca, but reflecting on what has been presented
to me by Ship Captain Don Alexandro Malaspina, head of the
expedition on which the commandants of the said goletas have
been engaged, they will observe that which follows.

12th   If it should be possible to make the stopover in San
Francisco that should be made in Monterey, and bearing in
mind that the almost continuous fog in that harbour makes it
difficult to map it without sacrificing considerable time, this
difficulty shall be balanced against the need for the said ships to
arrive in San Blas during November for the continuation of
their campaign on the coast of Nicaragua, looking on the
operation of mapping the said harbour [of San Francisco] as
useful but not necessary, and in such a case the stop in Monterey
would be convenient by reason of its good weather and abundance of provisions, serving also for the prompt restoration of
the seamen, who by then will need some rest.

13th   The goletas will follow the coast as far as the Cabo San
Lucas or mission of San José del Cabo, from which point they
will make for San Blas, and on their arrival their commandants
will give me a confidential report as extensive as possible on the

work they have carried out, since I know the difficulty, and that they must still be employed in the plotting of some maps on which there are data greatly needed for the true understanding of them.

14th   At the said Puerto de San Blas, I will direct to you the instructions necessary for the continuation of the campaign or Nicaragua voyage which the goletas referred to should carry out, and at that time their commandants will draw my attention to that which they believe suitable for the best attainment of this undertaking.

15th   The other divisions of the commission, as much political as physical can be found in detail in the instructions of Don Alexandro Malaspina which with my approval he has transmitted to the commandants of the said goletas, who will consider them complementary in all points which are not expressed here.

16th   Good treatment and harmony with the Indians is of the first importance, to establish in this way a solid friendship with them, so that our visits should not be as distressing as those of other voyagers to the detriment of humanity and the national credit. To facilitate this, the goletas will be provided with goods which are considered most appropriate to use as gifts to the Chiefs and people, in the discretion of the commanders. [These goods] can also serve in trade for supplies and to maintain in this way a commerce which will sustain friendship without expecting the gain or profit which they could produce.

17th   In dealing with the Indians, experience has proved that from time to time neither gifts nor sufferance will suffice to exempt oneself from their attacks, since a natural distrust reigns among them, springing from a lack of understanding of the reasons for the expeditions, especially those which are not commercial. For this reason the commandants of the goletas will not omit any precaution to cover themselves against surprise, making use of the superiority of their arms in those cases that necessity requires for their own security, but having always in mind that it is a last resort to [do anything] directly opposed to humanity, and it can only be justified by the need of self preservation.

18th   If while at sea, on the northwest coast, or in the Strait ships of other European nations are encountered, the commandants of the goletas will endeavour to observe the greatest accord with them, avoiding disputes which cause displeasure to their nations and delay the commission, and assisting each other reciprocally.

19th   For merchant ships of other nations, the said commandants are not obliged to maintain the respect due to ships of war, since the lack of force to secure these rights could cause disrespect for the flag, a voluntary concession of such privileges being preferable.

20th   If any warship or merchant ship of another nation has an intention of seizing the ships or making them undergo a forced search, the commandants will endeavour to escape from them by the best prudent means, and if this does not suffice to make what defence is permitted by their arms and forces.

Mexico, 31st January, 1792.

Part Three
The Voyage Narrative

THE VOYAGE NARRATIVE
I

A proposal is made to the Viceroy of New Spain for an expedition to examine the
Entrada de Juan de Fuca with the goletas Sutil *and* Mexicana: *They sail from the*
Puerto de San Blas to Acapulco, to make use of the assistance of the corvettes
Descubierta *and* Atrevida: *They are delayed and do not find the corvettes on their*
arrival: Defects of the goletas: The correction of the vital defects is started:
Difficulties in doing this: Unlimited help provided to the expedition by the
Viceroy: They are soon ready to set sail: Their manifest and rig.

His Majesty's corvettes *Descubierta* and *Atrevida* under the
command of Ship Captain Don Alejandro Malaspina[1] returned
to the Port of Acapulco at the end of October, 1791, having
spent the summer in an unsuccessful search for the supposed
passage to the Atlantic. The entrance of this passage should have
been in latitude 60° on the northwest coast of North America,
according to the well known account of Lorenzo Ferrer Maldonado. The corvettes had examined and located many points of
the coast from that latitude south, but there were some they
could not fix. The Commandant proposed to His Excellency
Count Revillagigedo, the Viceroy of New Spain, that an expedi-

---

[1] "Capitán de Navío." Ranks in the Real Armada corresponded approximately with those in
the British Royal Navy of that time as follows:

      Capitán de Navío-Post Captain
      Capitán de Fragata-Commander
      Teniente de Navío-Lieutenant [senior]
      Teniente de Fragata-Lieutenant [junior]
      Alférez de Navío-No exact equivalent.
      Alférez de Fragata-No exact equivalent.
Piloto [de primero clase]-Master.
"Alférez" is translated as "Ensign."

tion should be sent to locate the unverified points and to continue the examination of the Entrance of Juan de Fuca. He suggested sending Frigate Captains Dionisio Alcalá Galiano and Cayetano Valdés, in command of the goletas[2] *Sutil* and *Mexicana*, which had just been built at the dockyard at San Blas de California, taking as second in command Frigate Lieutenants Don Juan Vernacci and Secundino Salamanca.[3]

Part [of this expedition], the examination of Juan de Fuca, had already been decided on by the Viceroy, acting on the King's orders, and even as soon as the beginning of December he had decided to send the goleta *Sutil*[4] to undertake this. Considering that Don Alejandro Malaspina proposed an expedition with chronometers and instruments used by officers in whom he had confidence, the Viceroy agreed to this proposal, and agreed that the goletas should go from San Blas to Acapulco to prepare for the voyage under the direction and with the help of Don Alejandro Malaspina.

However, the goletas were delayed in their arrival at Acapulco. The seasonal fevers had made their presence felt to an epidemic degree and the season was becoming too advanced for the Plan of Operations which Malaspina had planned for the corvettes, so he left that harbour for the Phillipine Islands on the 20th of December, eight days before the arrival of the goletas. He left behind whatever he considered would be useful for the fitting out of these ships, under the impression that they would arrive equipped in the way their Commandants had requested in a note directed to the Commandant of the Department of San Blas, Ship Captain D. Juan de la Quadra. In that note, in addition to crew and equipment, they had indicated everything that appeared to them to be necessary to modify the rig of the goletas.

---

[2] "Goleta"; literally a schooner, but used to describe small ships regardless of their rig. See the Introduction.

[3] In the *Relación del Viage* as it was published in 1802, hereinafter cited as *Viage*, a summary of the Spanish explorations in 1774-5 and 1789-91 precedes this paragraph. Throughout this chapter, the voyage of Malaspina gets fuller treatment and the Viceroy gets more space in the *Viage* than in the manuscript.

[4] In fact, it was the *Mexicana* the Viceroy planned to send.

As soon as [the goletas] arrived at Acapulco, Galiano and Valdés proceeded to examine them, and the first thing that presented itself to view was their defective construction, by reason of the narrow beam. In addition to causing the poor stability experienced in such a short voyage, the narrow beam reduced the space in the hold so that it was found impossible to carry the water supply and provisions necessary for their voyage to Nutca, unless they followed the coast. This was a route that many ships had found impracticable because of adverse currents and winds.

In this situation, the Commandants thought of raising the decks of the goletas thirteen pulgadas[5] and giving them a different arrangement [of bulkheads] in order to increase their capacity. To remedy the loss of hull strength resulting from this work they would fit doubling planks three pulgadas[6] thick to a width of two pies[7] increasing the thickness of the wale[8] to four pulgadas.[9]

This plan being approved by the Viceroy, we got to work on the task on the 2nd of January, 1792, in spite of not having more than one carpenter and one caulker in the two goletas, both of the third class, and in spite of the shortage of tools in the ships. The Commandants, suffering all day the rigourous heat of the sun, tried to make up for the deficiency of workmen who could join in.[10] Their number consisted of local joiners, a caulker, and some Filipinos from the crew of the King's frigate *San Andrés* which was at that time in the harbour under the command of Frigate Lieutenant Don Joaquin Berenguer de Marquina. However, his carpenters and caulkers being occupied in the refitting of their own ship, could not be employed in the goletas during the months of January and February.

The meagre resources available to the commandants made the repairs more difficult at every step. The Commandant of the

---

[5] 30 cm. In the *Viage* the words "permitted by their hold" are added.

[6] 7 cm.   [7] 55 cm.

[8] "Cinta." A band of thicker planking running along the hull above its waterline.

[9] 9 cm.   [10] In the *Viage* this sentence is omitted.

Department of San Blas, busy in fitting out various vessels at the time of departure of the goletas, could not manage that they should come in the way the Commandants of the goletas requested. Thus, without wood, oakum, pitch, tools, or appropriate workmen, continuous difficulties were faced for some work, which [we] had been obliged to undertake only through necessity. Woodsmen were ordered to cut and transport the necessary pieces of timber. Three pit saws, all that could be found in Acapulco, were put in order, and the work on the goletas and the making of additional casks followed as quickly as possible. When resources were lacking, they turned to supplies found in the shops of the country and in the Royal warehouses, and to the Commandant of the Manila frigate, who in view of the need, helped with all the means possible in the circumstances.

These [means] were not the same as in other Royal ships. The Manila frigate was assigned and charged by the government to take the commercial goods ordered from Manila. For the development of the Phillipine Islands, the frigate had made directly for Acapulco from Manila. On his return to Manila the Commandant of the frigate had to account for the goods in his charge at a hearing by a Judge-Auditor of the Manila judiciary.[11] Since Marquina had no surplus of some supplies he had to give us only the indispensable goods unobtainable in any other way, leaving the charges to be covered by [approval at] his hearing.[12]

The goletas should have brought from San Blas provisions for six months for a crew of thirteen which had been planned there [for the Juan de Fuca expedition], even though the Commandants had informed [the officials of San Blas] otherwise. They came with only one [month's provisions]. Hoping to obtain these in Acapulco to the satisfaction [of the Comman-

---

[11] An "oidor" of the Manila "audiencia."

[12] "Residencia." An audit of the ships' inventories. For an explanation, see Petrie, 1971. Evidently this passage is intended to relieve Marquina of his responsibility for the goods. Galiano's intention was not realized. Correspondence in AGN Mar. 103 on this subject continues to December 1798.

dants, these officials] had asked the Commandant of the Department to contribute this assistance.

To give the maximum capacity, the two bread lockers [with] which [each ship] came were made into one and waterproofed. The planking was thin and the lockers not built as strongly as in larger ships. The bread at the bottom and sides was wet. It stank as soon as it was taken out and was discarded. Still, the portable soup[13] was of better quality, and the goletas had to carry excellent food, to prevent by all means imaginable the onset of diseases in ships which sailed devoid of medical facilities. The Viceroy approved the rejection of the [damaged] food and with unlimited assistance contributed to our taking as many antiscorbutics as we believed appropriate and as many presents and trade goods as we believed useful. He provided the Commandants with all the money and orders they requested, by means of which the goletas were fitted as appeared suitable to the benefit and performance of the Commission.

The bread lockers warranted all possible care to place them in a condition in which this valuable material[14] would not deteriorate. Thus, after tarring the lockers they were given a layer of tarred canvas and lined with tin, making two bread lockers capable of containing in each goleta sixty quintals[15] of bread in place of the thirty seven which they held formerly.

The goletas had come from San Blas with a rig halfway between schooner and brig, but the commandants not finding this suitable, Galiano fitted out *Sutil* entirely in the latter rig, and Valdés [fitted out] *Mexicana* in the former, by means of masts made from two rough cedar spars carried by the frigate *San Andrés* as topsail studding sail booms.[16]

---

[13] A mixture of vegetables and meat, boiled down until it was solid.

[14] i.e. the bread.　　　　　　　[15] 2750 kg.

[16] Evidently the goletas were rigged in San Blas as modified brigs, with both a square forecourse and a fore-and-aft one, the latter for sailing to windward. Drawings of *Mexicana* drawn by the expedition artist after it was dismasted and repaired at Nootka show that Valdés returned to the original rig. A studding sail is a narrow sail set on a boom extending outwards from the end of the yard carrying a square sail.

Also *Sutil* was supplied with a boat of nearly the full length between the masts, which was exchanged with the Ensign of the frigate *San Andrés* for a cedar[17] pinnace brought from San Blas, even though this reduced the advantage of avoiding weight or bulk on the deck, since the pinnace was of no use for the way in which it had to be employed. The boat brought by the *Mexicana* was so small and flimsy, that not in the end having time or opportunity to cut down a boat from the same frigate, Valdés preferred the pinnace left by *Sutil* to his own boat.[18]

The Colonel of the Regiment of the Puebla de los Angeles, Don José Manuel de Alava, who [held the office of] Governor in Acapulco, contributed as much as could be supplied from the stores in his warehouses, providing to the goletas besides other effects muskets, pistols, and sabres. There had arrived in both the [goletas] the weapons requested for each. Even these were unserviceable, since the attentions of the Department of San Blas on the departure of the goletas had been much superior to the means at the disposal of its Commandant. Also [the Governor in Acapulco] provided a medical attendant[19] taken from [among] the convicts who were going to the Phillipines in the frigate *San Andrés*, augmenting in this way the practical knowledge of surgery acquired by Vernacci and Salamanca and the books of family medicine they had been able to acquire.

On the 7th of March the frigate *San Andrés* left on a good breeze for Manila. The work had made the goletas ready [for sea], manned, prepared through their work, and [in the process of] embarking their effects as rapidly as possible, to make sail the next day in the state shown in the manifests.[20]

---

[17] "Cedro." This word usually meant a hardwood, but the species differed in different places.

[18] This paragraph omitted from the *Viage*.

[19] "Sangrador," literally a leech.

[20] The manifests are not included in MN MS 619, but appear in the nearly identical AGN Hist. 558. See Appendix 2. The *Viage* includes an extract of the manifest.

II

Voyage from Acapulco to the Puerto de Nutca: The goletas drop down to twelve degrees of latitude because of light winds and their poor windward performance: Mexicana is dismasted, losing its mainmast: While the damage is being repaired they are driven towards the coast, and the voyage is delayed: With favourable winds the goletas arrive at Nutca.

The breeze was awaited throughout the morning of the 8th [of March], the time being used to stow cargo. The officers were anxious to make sail as well as to rest from the fatigue they had endured in harbour. There was a suggestion of a breeze towards half past one in the afternoon and immediately the goletas weighed anchor and sailed close hauled on the starboard tack on a rising west wind. They soon demonstrated their poor sailing qualities, and the inefficiency of the sails. At sunset they were about two leagues[1] from the harbour entrance. There followed winds from WSW to WNW and the goletas sailed close hauled until the 18th to get away from the coast and seek the tropical winds.[2] With moderate winds, they lost latitude down to the twelfth degree without having gained more than 2° 51' of longitude to the west.[3] The wind had been fair, and the bottoms had been given a coating of tallow, but the goletas never exceeded three knots sailing close hauled, and in consequence the leeway was very great.

---

[1] Six nautical miles. [2] The northeast trade winds.

[3] [Footnote in the MS.] Longitude is reckoned from the meridian of Acapulco which is taken as 16° 50' of latitude and 93° 45' west of Cádiz.

From the 18th the winds veered to the north and a course in the fourth quadrant[4] could be made. In order not to waste the season, continuous attempts were made to change the stowage [in order to improve the trim], carrying as much sail as possible, with the edge of the deck almost always under water. The winds, even though they were not heavy, were usually fresh from the north to northeast, in spite of which we could not attain the latitude of Acapulco until the 29th with the advantage of 15° [of west longitude] gained on this parallel. Comparing our voyage with that of the corvettes during the previous year,[5] we found we required double the time according to the calculation we made, and needed to double our progress. On this day we suffered the misfortune of disabling the marine barometer which had been secured to the mainmast rigging through not having an appropriate place to put it.

On the 31st, angular distances from the moon to the sun were taken, verifying the confidence we could place in the chronometers, finding the longitude to be within a quarter of a degree of that indicated [by the chronometers]. The goletas yawed too much to hold a course and one could not count on the estimates,[6] [to give our position] and thus we relied on [the lunar distance calculation] at the point of observation.

The winds did not start to veer from the northeast towards east until the 5th of April. [We were at that time] at 20° 48' of latitude and 21° 30' of longitude. Two days later they backed from northeast to north until the 11th when they veered again to the east, continuing to ease so that two days later we experienced them for the first time from the southeast. We found ourselves at this time in 26° 4' of latitude and 27° 20' of longitude. Consequently the voyage was much delayed, partly by lighter winds than could be expected, and

---

[4] i.e to the north of the west.

[5] *Descubierta* and *Atrevida*, commanded by Alejandro Malaspina; all the officers except Galiano had been on this voyage to Alaska, which had included a visit to the Spanish establishment at Nootka.

[6] Estimates of course and speed, known as dead reckoning in maritime usage.

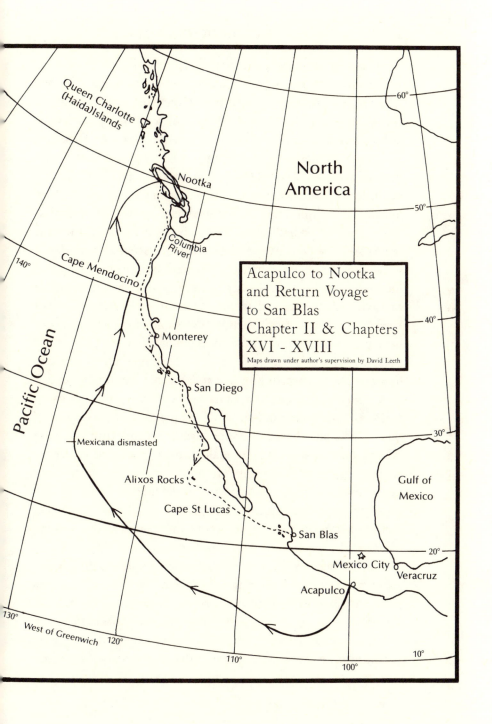

Queen Charlotte (Haida) Islands

Nootka

North America

Columbia River

140°

Cape Mendocino

Pacific Ocean

Monterey

60°

50°

40°

Acapulco to Nootka
and Return Voyage
to San Blas
Chapter II & Chapters
XVI - XVIII

Maps drawn under author's supervision by David Leeth

San Diego

30°

Mexicana dismasted

Alixos Rocks

Gulf of
Mexico

Cape St Lucas

San Blas

20°

Mexico City

Veracruz

Acapulco

130°

West of Greenwich   120°

110°

10°

100°

partly by the previously mentioned characteristics of the ships.

On the 14th we repeated the lunar observations with the satisfaction of finding the results in agreement with those of the chronometers within half a degree [of longitude]. We were sailing this day with studding sails set with the hope of starting to recover the delays of the voyage, but at two in the afternoon disaster overtook us when *Mexicana* broke its mainmast six and one half feet below the head. This accident presented itself at first in a bad light, making us unable to attain our arrival at Nutca, where we had to sail to take on board some provisions which were to be conveyed from San Blas, and also to obtain some indispensable assistance to proceed to the examination [of the Strait of Juan de Fuca]. The supplies that the goletas carried, and even those that could be acquired in Acapulco, had been used in their reconstruction. We found ourselves with very little pitch, no oakum, and a shortage of other stores with the exception of nails. For these reasons, it became more necessary to go to Nutca, precluding our making for any other place.[7]

As soon as *Mexicana* was dismasted, *Sutil* came to under eased topsails. The Commandant of *Mexicana* said in passing *Sutil* that he had no other damage, except the dismasting. Galiano said to him that he should make whatever course he found convenient, steering for any safe port, and *Sutil* should follow astern until the wind lulled and he could send over a carpenter to repair the damage. Valdés replied that he would make for Nutca and at once went to work to secure the stump of the mast to continue the voyage.

The southerly wind blew up with a heavy sea, and during the night veered to the west with squalls and threatening weather. *Mexicana* ran off at ten points from the wind[8] with a great spread of sail, to make the ship secure, and to be able to carry out the task of affixing cleats to the mainmast to attach the rigging. For this they made sheer legs from the goleta's oars, and at the

---

[7] This sentence is omitted from the *Viage*.

[8] That is, with the wind somewhat behind the ship. Eight points equal ninety degrees.

Sutil leads the way, followed by *Mexicana*
A drawing made after the dismasted *Mexicana* had been re-rigged at Nootka.
The location not known, but possibly in the San Juan Islands,
with Mount Baker in the distance.

Courtesy of Museo Naval, Madrid.

cost of much risk and fatigue, as can be imagined, the mast was secured by dawn on the 15th and ready to carry the mainsail in any contrary wind and lie to it to continue the voyage to Nutca.

For three days the wind blew from the west to the southwest. The heavy sea from the southwest did not permit the launching of a boat. *Mexicana* constantly maintained a course ten points off the wind with the help of its mainsail. At last the sea eased and the carpenter went over to *Mexicana* [on the 18th] to work on making cross-trees for the mainmast, in order to put up a topmast, which, with its yard, was passed over from *Sutil* the next afternoon. On the 21st at seven in the morning *Mexicana* was situated with its topsail drawing, ready to continue the navigation not far behind *Sutil*, having had the good fortune to gain 9° 30′ of latitude during the days it was delayed while the damage was being repaired.

The accident of dismasting did not entail any setback other than [the goletas] having fallen away from the route. At times they were forced off the direct course they had intended to follow, and fell to leeward towards the coast, approaching to within fifty three leagues.[9] In consequence, if fresh winds from the west to northwest had followed, the voyage to Nutca would have been much longer. For this [reason] a course of NW 8° W was set when the wind permitted, to gain longitude, but the wind was not so favourable that we could follow this course at all times. It continued from W to WSW until the 27th. The goletas constantly sailed close hauled, but the current, which had approached one mile per hour along the coast according to the chronometers, brought the ships to within twenty leagues of the coast at 41° 58′ of latitude.

From this day until the 2nd of May winds were light and variable from the third and fourth quadrants[10] and we adopted the tack which would lead away from the coast, trying at the same time not to lose latitude. Coastal pilots of these waters recommend strongly that to assure the voyage, it should be

---

[9] 160 nautical miles.   [10] From south to west to north.

made in the meridian 28° west of San Blas or 33° 20′ west of Acapulco, and no nearer to the coast, taking for granted [that] the wind [would be] from the northwest. We had experienced many variations in the wind, a circumstance [which led us to] forsake the route which was proposed to us. In practice, our success had reassured us about our system, which we preferred.[11]

On the 2nd of May in 43° degrees of latitude and 29° 30′ of longitude, the wind settled in the southwest and south. On the 4th the winds veered to the fourth quadrant[12] but were light and suitable for sailing close hauled. On the 7th our good fortune returned with southerly winds until we reached 46° of latitude and 30° 20′ of longitude, coming always from our stern until [we reached] Nutca, notwithstanding that we had to follow various courses. The [preferred] route slants towards the coast to Nutca from 47° latitude, inclining towards the course of our approach, under the assurance that the longitude deduced from the chronometers was appropriate, and confirmed by lunar observations.

At daybreak on the 12th of May, we were in view of the Cabo Frondoso, in its meridian.[13] We sailed all day and night under a clear sky and easy wind. [We were] in view of the port at daybreak [on May 13], from which came the Chief or Tais[14] Macuina in a canoe, to be received in the goletas with his relatives and friends. We presented to him an axe, four knives, and some other pieces of hardware. He immediately recognized Valdés, Vernacci, and Salamanca, who had been in the corvettes[15] during the previous year, and embraced them with evidence of the greatest pleasure. He asked for his friends Malaspina, Bustamante, and their officers, and remained in the goletas until [they reached] the anchorage. *Sutil* touched the rocks near the mouth of the harbour but was freed in a

---

[11] The *Viage* adds that they became aware of the mistake of the "coastal pilots."

[12] West to north.   [13] Due south of it.

[14] "Tais," an approximation of the Indian word for a chief, appears at a number of places in the manuscript, and is left untranslated.

[15] Malaspina's ships.

few minutes without the least damage. Assisted by boats and launches that were in the port, both of us entered under tow and anchored at two o'clock in the afternoon.[16]

---

[16] The *Viage* adds two paragraphs of recommendations for planning a similar voyage, including a statement that a ship can anchor outside the harbour.

III

Ships which were at Nutca: Refitting of the goletas: The corvette Aránzazu *arrives: Harmonious relations with the Indians: We are unable to advance our knowledge of their customs: Some impressions we could acquire: The French frigate* Flavia *arrives: Summary of the observations at Nutca.*

We found the corvette *Concepción* anchored and rigged down in the port, under the command of Ship Lieutenant Don Francisco de Elisa, who was living ashore as commandant of a provisional establishment which we had maintained there since the beginning of 1790. In addition the frigate of war *Santa Gertrudis* was in the port under the command of Ship Captain Don Alonso Torres, also the brig[1] *Activa* commanded by Pilot Don Salvador Menendez, these vessels having left the port of San Blas on the 1st of March of this year. The frigate had arrived on the 29th of April, and the brig on the 4th of May, after having put back to repair some damage which occurred a few days after its departure.[2] In charge of both the establishment and the ships was Ship Captain Don Juan de la Bodega y Quadra who had come in the *Gertrudis* with the objective of putting into effect the treaty of convention made by our Court with that of England [to settle the disputes that had occurred] in 1789.[3]

---

[1] Or brigantine; there was no distinction between the two in either Spain or England in the eighteenth century.

[2] The *Viage* omits the account of the voyage.

[3] The words in brackets are inserted in MN MS 619 in a different handwriting. They do not appear in AGN Hist 558. The dispute arose when Esteban Martínez seized some ships belonging to a syndicate headed by the British fur trader John Meares.

[Bodega y Quadra] had orders from the Viceroy of New Spain to provide the goletas with any assistance that was required, but the small resources at his disposal and his many preoccupations made him unable to refit the goletas with the expedition we wished. We reduced our needs to:

-Changing the principal working lines, since those we had brought were continually failing because of the poor quality of the cordage.

-Making use of the opportune assistance of the frigate *Santa Gertrudis*, which since it came from the Department of Cádiz had cordage of excellent quality.

-Providing each goleta from this cordage with a hawser five pulgadas thick to serve as an anchor cable.[4]

-Making a mainmast and a foremast for *Mexicana*.

-Reinforcing its crossjack and topsail yards.

-Providing a launch for *Mexicana*, made by cutting down from the stern a boat from *Concepción*.

-Reinforcing *Sutil's* boom and repairing its boat.

-Providing the two goletas with tar, tallow, pitch, and other necessary tools that were lacking.

-Adding [to the crew] in *Sutil* two Marines, a leading gunner, and a caulker, a seaman to replace one who was sick, and in *Mexicana* a carpenter and three soldiers of the Company of Don Pedro Alberni[5] who had been in the guard of the corvette *Concepción*.

On the 13th [of May] the corvette *Aránzazu* arrived, which came from San Blas to carry out explorations to the north. This vessel brought some supplies for the goletas which we had requested from San Blas to replace those consumed or damaged; but not having any damaged [supplies] we took only those we had consumed, with some additions, leaving the rest at the disposal of the Commandant, Don Quadra.[6]

---

[4] Five pulgadas is about 12 cm. This seems excessive for a ship the size of *Sutil* or *Mexicana*. If the MS read "in circumference," rather than "thick," the cable would be of the right size.

[5] The Catalonian Volunteers.

While we were in Nutca, we were particularly gratified to see the close friendship which prevailed between the Spanish and the Indians. Moved by the gifts and good treatment of the commandant, Macuina had come to live very close to the ships. He ate nearly every day from the table of the commandant. Although he was not at the table, he was very close to it. He used a knife and fork like the most polite European, letting the servants wait on him, and himself contributing to the good humour of the society. He would drink wine with pleasure, and it was necessary to advise moderation in this liquor, which he called "water of Spain," so that he would not become intoxicated.[7] Ordinarily, his brother Cuatlazapé accompanied him, to whom he would show the greatest affection. Also, some relatives and his subordinates were in the habit of eating in the room. For the latter a plate of either navy or kidney beans was provided daily, food they preferred above anything else. Macuina was gifted with a clear and bright intelligence, and knew well his rights of sovereignty. He complained a great deal about the treatment [of Indians] by foreign ships which trafficked along the coast, because of several outrages which he said his people had received. He denied the ceding of the port to the English Lieutenant Meares, and only admitted having permitted him to establish himself in it, continually repeating the concession he had made to the King of Spain of the port of Nutca and the beaches thereof with all their produce.[8]

We do not give a description of the discovery and [development of the] port of Nutca and our establishment in it, nor the dress of the Indians, because it has already been done in the description of the voyage of Alejandro Malaspina, and thus we only describe the ideas we could acquire and the incidents we

---

[6] This paragraph of the manuscript contains a number of alterations in another hand, none altering the sense. The original has been followed, being more intelligible. The *Viage* omits all but the first sentence.

[7] The *Viage* reads that Macuina left to others the care of limiting the quantity of wine that he drank.

[8] The ethnological material in the paragraphs which follow is omitted from the *Viage*.

observed. Our attention and presence being directed solely to the immediate surroundings of the goletas, we had no opportunity for investigations, but we willingly accepted the loss of such an opportunity on seeing the expedition of the commandant Quadra furnished with intelligent individuals whose sole object was a philosophical examination of those lands, and for whom an uninterrupted residency will provide the means to perform this duty with all satisfaction. We hoped that in case their reports should not be published, they would provide for our acquiring them. We would take from them everything we consider useful and do due justice to the author.[9]

These savages live principally by fishing, not omitting to make use of the sustenance they get from fruits, wild roots, and game. From this last source venison at times is one of the major foods, and in the fishery the whale is the most appreciated, either because they prefer it to other fish, or because its size gives them the means of satisfying their hunger. Cuatlazapé, the brother of Macuina, boasted of being the one devoted to the fishing of this ferocious animal. He achieved his objective of capturing it at the cost of much risk, making use of his canoes, a harpoon which he threw with a rope, and a buoy to indicate the direction of the animal after it was wounded, and as soon as it was dead, the location of its end.

The classes which could be distinguished were the chiefs or rulers they call Taises and the subjects who are called mischismis [sic].[10] Three of the first class who could be distinguished were Macuina, Tlupananul, and Cicomacsia, all heads of tribes. After the other [taises], their closest relatives could be distinguished. The right of sovereignty is hereditary, and even passes to sons as soon as they have attained the full vigour of manhood

---

[9] Galiano is referring to the scientist José Mariano Moziño, the anatomist José Maldonado, and the artist Atanasio Echeverría, who had been sent with Quadra for the specific purpose of making scientific studies, including an ethnography of Nutca. See: Moziño, Wilson.

[10] Galiano's word "vasallos" is translated here as "subjects"; having identified this as the meaning of the Indian word "mischismi" Galiano uses "mischismi" thereafter. Word untranslated in later references.

Casique Pral de Nutca nombrado Maquina

Macuina, the principal chief at Nootka
During the years he cornered the fur trade, he achieved
a ten-fold increase in price.
Courtesy of Museo Naval, Madrid.

and their fathers are in their decline, as verified by two others. In fact, the male succession to Macuina could fail, since he has an only daughter, called Apenas. He was negotiating a marriage between her and the heir of Uicaninish, a powerful tais and ruler of the territory immediately to the southeast, called Claucuad.[11] If this happens, with the tais of Claucuad already respected for his forces and riches, he [Macuina] will be able to subjugate all the nearby lands.[12]

The taises are masters of the life and labour of their mischismis, distributing work to them and having whatever they acquire at their disposal. [The taises] respect the right of ownership as the first principle of good order, and [enjoy] the affection of their subjects which arises from the best of treatment and from interest in their well being. The taises can hold various women, the mischismis only one, using all of them only at the full moon.[13]

They are so afraid of contravening this point of religion, particularly the taises, that they believe death will ensue if they breach it. Macuina said that his father had been one of the victims of such a breach of order. In spite of this there are the same vices in this society as in those more civilized. They guard their women jealously, but not to the extent of that they go against their own interest or do not make use of their strength. Some [women] dedicate themselves also to taking those not their own, taking their gratification from them without the least reserve, if they are not married. Macuina had four wives, and distinguished as his favourite one of ordinary looks named Clasiacá.

They recognize a Supreme Tais who lives in Heaven and is called Cuautle; they consider him a beneficial God, Creator, and Preserver of all things. They presume as well other lesser gods whom they respect, abominate, or love according to their

---

[11] Now Clayuquot Sound.

[12] This is the first place in the narrative that can be compared to the notes in MN MS 330. See: Introduction. These notes say that Apenas was the older daughter of Macuina.

[13] Moziño wrote that the full moon restriction applied only to chiefs.

evil or goodness. They believe in the immortal soul, but limit predestination to the taises, who Macuina said, would be happy in Heaven in the company of Cuautle, body and soul, if their deeds have been pleasing to him, but if they should have offended [Cuautle] their bodies would be eaten by dogs, without this punishment extending to their souls, which are predestined to enjoy the company of Cuautle. Not so those of the mischismis; these can never merit the good fortune to go to Heaven, because they are destined to go towards the centre of the earth.

Also, the Supreme Tais lends his beneficent ears to the earthly taises. All the mischismis of Nutca have the greatest confidence in the prayers of Macuina, and this deference ensures them of consideration and respect. Macuina has a seat covered with painted figures of outlandish animals and from it he cries out to Cuautle in times of scarcity or calamity with mournful chants and entreaties, at times keeping vigil all night. His wives and family keep some distance away, out of view, responding from time to time to his prayers.

The people of Nutca have a singular tradition, which Macuina related in this way: Cuautle created Woman and finding her to be alone and distressed he took pity on her and came in a copper canoe to an island on which she lived. The astonished woman rushed to see the wonder, increased her cries and blew her nose. Cuautle comforted her, telling her to preserve this excretion because from it would come her companion. The woman complied with this command and in effect a tiny child resulted who grew little by little until arriving at manhood. To this story, invented by some venerated old man or woman, they accord the creation of their first ancestors and the propagation of the human species.[14]

To us, favoured by the revelations of the Enlightenment, it is easy to explain physically one question formerly so much disputed. Geographical knowledge has led to the removal of the

---

[14] This is a brief summary of a legend still told by the Mowachaht elders.

veil of obscurity covering the manner in which the human species was propagated on this coast. The closeness [of the coast] to that of Asia in its northern part, the similarity of the inhabitants from one to another place, and the existence of communities all the way from the north to the south with many similar customs, leads to admitting without the slightest contradiction an idea that what happened was that the first inhabitants crossed from Asia by Bering Strait or in its vicinity, extending afterwards to the south as required by the circumstance of having to find food along the shores.

We did not find any particular difference in the facial features whereby to characterize the sexes. The most notable is that of the voice, which is thinner in the women. [The natives] consider it a distinction to be a male. Twice we came across two men squatting as usual, in which position they were covered by their cloaks. Asked if they were women, they stood up as if offended, to demonstrate their sex, on which subject they tried to investigate ourselves in every imaginable way.

In spite of the exaggerated estimates made by Captain Meares of the number of Macuina's subjects we did not place the number at more than four thousand, who roam seasonally around the different villages from the inlets leading in from the Boca de Buena Esperanza to the entry at Nutca, to escape, in sheltered places, the risks of winter, as well as to provide themselves with sustenance which in that season the sea at times denies them. To supply this need they cure fish dried in smoke or by the wind, but painful scarcities are still commonly suffered.

As indicated by their understanding of the creation of man, described above, and the use of copper by Cuautle, they value this metal highly. Even if it is old, they prefer it to all other metals. This can be compared to the way in which, among us, gold and silver are used as the general standard of values. They hold iron in much less esteem than copper. Under a shed where casks were made for the ships, there were some pieces of hoops of this metal, which did not excite the greed of the Indians to a point where particular caution was necessary. While we could affirm that the inclination to thievery attributed to them by travellers had nearly disappeared, this was not because of any moral superiority over Europeans. The orders established by Macuina and his rigourous penalties had contributed to their respect for the sacred rights of property. This tais, and also the mischismis, had established their good faith on various occasions, asking for the loan of sheets of copper from our establishment valued at a certain number of [sea otter] pelts, to trade with the Nuchimases,[15] and on their return from their voyage completing their contracts exactly.

The purposes of their wars are contention for land and the adjacent seas, and making themselves masters of the mischismis. Their arms were formerly knives and bows and arrows; now they add what they can of ours. They have had continuous peace during the time of our establishment, and one can attribute their having enjoyed this advantage, which they know as one of the greatest, to their respect for our arms. It is believed that some prisoners resulting from war had been destined by the victors to be sacrificed and used for food. In this respect travellers with incontrovertible facts categorized them as cannibals, but[16] in the time that their actions were under our examination there were no signs or word of such horrible cruelty. We tried to make Macuina and all his subjects regard [cannibalism] thus, advising them that if they committed [this cruelty] they would forego all our friendship and good treatment and we would rigourously punish anyone proven guilty of such an abominable offence. Europeans who trade with barbarous nations and bring to them all the evils of civilization making them acquainted with many things of which they gain considerable knowledge, must try to recompense them with whatever physical and moral benefits lie within their reach.[17]

---

[15] Nimpkish Indians.

[16] MS 619 uses "por que" [because]; AGN 558 uses "pero" [but], which fits the context.

Quicomacsia invited us to his village on the 20th of May to give us a dance. The village was up the inlet at the place they call Maluinas.[18] This tais is the same who in the previous year had called himself Quicsiocomic, who by a new marriage with the daughter of a tais of the Nuchimases had changed his name to another which, as we understood it, carried more weight. We could never understand the difference, but he was proud of his alliance, of which he boasted as a circumstance which placed him above Macuina.[19] He said he was Tais of Nutca and Nuchimas, and therefore superior to Macuina. The dance took place to the sound of the noise of small sticks which they broke off from tree branches, and with which they beat on planks. Quicomacsia disguised himself, first with feathers, then representing various animals, among which one was an imitation of a bear walking at times on four feet and acting as if pursued by a hunter. After this extraordinary spectacle, he placed himself across from us at some distance, and naming each of us individually in a loud voice, had otter skins brought to us. On another day he came to see us on the goletas. Being prepared for his arrival with the object of receiving presents, we gave them to him. He told us that he did not receive the gifts in trade, because chiefs do not trade but make reciprocal gifts. To stimulate us to increase the value of our presents, he repeated his claimed precedence over Macuina.

This vanity of ennobling themselves over the others is the principal topic of conversation of the taises. Tlupananul, equalizing two fingers of his hand, said to us that he was Cococoa Macuina.[20] We did not observe that they had the least respect for each other in their communications. If Tlupananul did not appear satisfied with the preference given by the Commandant

[17] This is the end of the ethnological material omitted from the *Viage*.

[18] Sometimes given as Malvinas.

[19] The notes in MN MS 330, say the new name reflected his connection with the Nuchimases through his marriage.

[20] Sic. "Cococoa" is an adjective in the language of the Mowachaht Indians, meaning similar or like. See: Kendrick, 1985, Appendix.

Quadra to Macuina, usually he recalled the services performed with his great canoe to the corvettes and to the [Spanish] establishment [at Nutca], and his continued gifts; but in this [generosity] he was not inferior to Macuina who, noticing that Elisa was short of provisions before the ships arrived, ordered his mischismis to provide fish to our establishment, which they did repeatedly without asking to receive any compensation. Nonetheless, Tlupananul continued to come once a week, nearly always bringing to Commandant Quadra a deer. He ate close to the table, on the opposite side to Macuina; his vocabulary was limited, his manner stupid, but he showed an evident honesty.

On the 22nd [of May] two canoes of Indians came from Claucuad. In the principal one came a brother of Uicaninish to see Macuina, who he said was a relative. Everyone considered Macuina to be sovereign of the coast from the Entrada de Buena Esperanza to the Punta de Arrecifes with all the inlets inside. Thus, even though we did not observe any decided submissiveness in Quicomacsia, and much less in Tlupananul, to some extent a feudal system of government must be inferred, with some dependency. The Indians in the Claucuad canoes were very fat and [had] an appearance notably superior to the Nutcas. Among them the tais could be distinguished by his most valiant personage. They came provided with muskets and powder, because Uicaninish had acquired many arms in trading his peltries to Europeans, whose desire for profit led them into the imprudence of forming a considerable power in the dominions of Uicaninish. Still, as long as they did not break the laws of probity, ships which arrived there could count on finding in the Indians of this coast the best treatment and welcome, bearing in mind that one must always study their situation and actions, because although the taises try to maintain the best order, at times a dispute arising from not understanding the language or attempting to take satisfaction from an annoying mischismi can bring the most fatal consequences. We gave presents to the

Indians of Claucuad, and offered that if time permitted, we would accept the invitation they gave us to pay a visit to Uicaninish. What they asked for most was powder, showing in this that their defense and martial power merited their primary attention.

On the 26th, a ship came into view, and the flag was raised at the fort. Sighting this [the ship] approached the port, and the boat of *Santa Gertrudis* put out to direct it into the entry. It was the French frigate *La Flavia* of about five hundred tons burthen. Its captain, Mr. Magon, carried the new national flag, which we saw for the first time. His purpose was to trade for peltries on the coast, then proceed to the Asian coast to sell them, and to initiate enquiries for news of the unfortunate expedition of the Count of La Peyrouse,[21] to assist it in whatever eventuality was found. This point appeared to us very secondary in view of the route which they had undertaken.

During the time of our residence at Nutca the weather was very changeable. Still, stormy winds from the south prevailed, with rain and heavy storm clouds as though the winter had not entirely ended. Because of this, the emergence of the first satellite of Jupiter could not be observed on the night of the 16th, and although there was an opportunity on the 18th, full confidence could not be placed [in the observation] because the sun was only 7° below the horizon.[22]

A successful observation was made at 8 hours 30 minutes 20 seconds true time, giving a longitude of 120° 30′ 30″ west of Cádiz.[23] We stood by to repeat the observation on the 25th

---

[21] Lapérouse was the leader of a French voyage of exploration, who disappeared with his ships and all his men in the South Pacific early in 1789.

[22] The purpose of these observations, which could be taken only ashore, using a telescope on a fixed base, was to correct the chronometers, and hence determine longitude. This was done by observing some celestial phenomenon for which the time was known at a reference point. The observatory at Cádiz was the reference point used by Spain. There were no standard time zones until after the middle of the nineteenth century. In order to see the satellites of Jupiter, darkness was required. With the sun only 7° below the horizon, it would not have been fully dark.

but rainy weather prevented this important observation, [required] to establish exactly the longitude of Nutca. During the previous year it had not been possible for the corvettes to make [a longitude estimate] other than by lunar distances. The latitude of Nutca had been established as 49° 35′ 16″, and in repeating this we found only 4″ of difference, more to the north.[24] On the 28th the emergence of the second [satellite of Jupiter] was observed, with a difference of 19′ more to the west than the satellite observation of the 16th. The chronometers were judged to be satisfactory, the small one being preferable. The barometers could not be set up because the tubes were broken. The thermometers registered from 14 to 17,[25] and the eudiometer gave the following results:

	1st experiment	2nd experiment
The air in the main room in the Commandant's house	60 parts	53 parts
The open air	54	52
The hospital ward	54	52

The first experiment was made on the 28th, the sky being cloudy and the wind very slight from WSW, and the thermometer at 17.[26]

---

[23] The correct longitude is 126° 37′ 02″ west of Greenwich, or about 120° 20′ west of Cádiz. The error was mostly due to errors in the tables Galiano was using, according to the *Viage*.

[24] The correct latitude of the Spanish observatory is 49° 35′ 32″.

[25] Specified later to be degrees on the Reaumur scale. Add 25% to get degrees Celsius.

[26] A eudiometer is an instrument for measuring the concentration of gasses. The numbers seem to have been regarded as an expression of air purity, but the Fontana apparatus they were using was unreliable. Even if it had given correct results, a higher number would indicate a lower proportion of oxygen in the air.

The Harbor at Núñez Gaona

At right is the frigate *Princesa*. Just astern is *Mexicana* with *Sutil* on the left, carrying Galiano's command pennant.

Courtesy of Museo de América, Madrid.

IV

The goletas leave Nutca, and turn back because of bad weather: Attack by an American ship on the Indians of the Boca de Buena Esperanza: Evidence of the good character of Macuina: The goletas repeat their departure, and arrive at the Puerto de Núñez Gaona at the entrance of Juan de Fuca where they find the frigate Princesa.

On the 2nd of June, even though the flood tide was running [against us], we weighed at four in the morning, sailing on the land breeze from the north, and in fair weather. The narrowness of the port, and the need to round the Punta de Arrecifes required that the departure be made at dawn, to get clear before the land breeze died. The launches of the anchored vessels towed us outside the points [at the port entrance] and we made full sail after hoisting in our boats, laying our course at SW 1/4 S to clear the mentioned point and make our [onward] course on the [wind] shift to the west that regularly came in between ten o'clock and noon.

We had not gone far when the wind changed from east to south. We followed the tack to the WSW, and at ten thirty in the morning we tacked to the ESE, counting on the tide, which would be with us until two in the afternoon, and some easing of the wind direction, to enable us to clear the point and its shoal, even though the point lay dead ahead.

Increasingly threatening weather ensued, the sky began to

cloud over with a dark scud, and the land was covered with storm clouds. The wind, which turned to the SE, began to strengthen, to the point that at four thirty in the afternoon we turned towards the port with the intention of returning to it if the weather, which during the days before our departure we had observed to be very variable, did not clear. Next the storm clouds increased, it started to rain without intermission, and the southeaster got worse. These circumstances placed us in need of making for our former anchorage, which we attained at eight in the evening with the greatest relief.

The night which followed was cruel; the storm clouds thickened, the wind and rain continued, with the greatest violence and strength. We considered it fortunate that we had managed to get back, since otherwise we would have had one of the most critical nights the mariner can experience.

On the following day, June 3rd, the weather stayed the same. Macuina, who came to keep us company as was his habit, said to us in that language accompanied by action in the way that his talent made expressive, that we had not made our departure at an opportune time, and that, [if we] left [matters] in his care, he would determine [the proper time] with the utmost certainty. We accepted his offer, believing that the Indians who lived by the fishery, with vessels as vulnerable to misfortune as their canoes must, like our best fishermen, have observed the weather a great deal, so much that they understood it. However, he indicated that his prayers to Cuautle gave him a greater confidence than his knowledge, and in the Commandant's own house, he intoned them with the greatest devotion. We could not understand any words but "Cuautle" and "clus nas", which are "God" and "good weather." Since his intonation and face made us laugh, Macuina showed his annoyance, and it was necessary to satisfy him by telling him that we laughed at the tone, and through not having heard it [before]. The mischismis who were present listened to him with the greatest devotion, reproving us with their actions that we did not imitate him, and giving us to understand that we could expect good success from the prayers of their tais, as they had experienced continually.

On this day a canoe came asking Commandant Quadra for help against a ship which in the Boca de Buena Esperanza had attacked an Indian village, killing seven, wounding others, and dispossessing the rest of them of the [sea otter] skins they had. An injured man came in order that the surgeon might look after him, and Macuina intervened with Quadra so that [the surgeon] could take care of the wounded man, and that Quadra would proceed to punish the agressors. [1] According to our understanding the ship was the American corvette named *Columbia* under Captain Gray, [2] whom the Indians described by the sign that he had only one eye, which we knew. The motive they gave us was that not having wanted to agree to the sale of pelts to the Europeans, he had made use of force to compel them.

The large amount of copper that competing ships had traded on this coast had been the cause of a drop in its exchange value. The merchant who came to trade without knowing this calculated on the [basis of the] value it formerly had, to provide his cargo of pelts. He would arrive to trade and find that the Indians had raised the price of pelts, and [that] under the rate of exchange desired [by the Indians] great losses would ensue. These merchants, believing their operations could not be investigated, set aside moral questions and resorted to force for their profits. To this can be attributed the harm caused to the Indians by the ship in Boca de Buena Esperanza. If the governments of ships which trade on this coast do not impose severe penalties on those who breach the laws of probity, and offer rewards to those who denounce the perpetrators, they cover themselves with the greatest opprobrium. We can affirm that the Indians of Nutca are incapable of attacking any ship which arrives off their

[1] MS 330 says that the surgeon removed two balls from the wounded man's thigh.

[2] In fact, the attack was made by William Brown, an English fur trader. AGN Hist. 70.

shores, since all, without excepting Macuina, hold the greatest respect for the arms of the Old World.

Another new proof of the dignity and good character of Macuina came to us during this stay in Nutca. For the rape of a child who had not reached the age of puberty, one of his mischismis had been sentenced to death, the established penalty for such a crime. To avoid this punishment he had taken refuge in the frigate *Gertrudis*, asking the commandant Quadra to intercede for him with Macuina. Quadra did this, and Macuina, weighing this with a wry face, said to him that he would spare the [culprit's] life, as long as he stayed with the Spaniards, and had no further dealings with his people, but demanding that if in an equal case any Spaniard should take refuge in his power, [Quadra] would have to pardon him, if Macuina considered it fitting. Macuina asked for the clothing of the delinquent, who he said should dress as a European. Next, the Indian came to him, trembling to present himself to his tais, but [Macuina] treated him with a benevolence worthy of the most noble heart.

We can also affirm, to the honour of Macuina, that having ordered the punishment of death to another of his mischismis, he came to the *Gertrudis*, and left word that justice should be done while he was on board, showing the greatest emotion at being obliged to exercise severity to contain crime, and [showing] that he never diminished by his actions the character of an amiable Prince who looked on his subjects as sons.[3]

On the 4th [of June] the weather cleared, and at midday we went to Macuina; he told us that now the weather was safe, and that at night we could take our departure. In the afternoon we made a visit to his house, which was near the port. He received us with the greatest attention, presenting us with dried salmon and whale meat, saying to us that we could not eat some of his food without disgust and nausea, and similarly he with ours. He

---

[3] The *Viage* attaches the rape of the child to this episode, and adds a request by Macuina that the Spaniards should provide assistance to the man's family. MN MS 330 is similar. The *Viage* also adds a further eulogy of Macuina which does not appear in MS 330.

made fun of our delicacy with his actions, and to placate him we ate some raw salmon and Valdés even hastened to chew a piece of whale.

This house, which he had built to live near our establishment, was fifteen paces long and ten wide, and like the poops of the ships had had the improvement of some windows. In it were several chests, sheets of copper, and at the side opposite to where he was, several women were cooking fish in a square [wooden][4] vessel with a sewn flat bottom, pitched to prevent the escape of boiling water through the seams. We examined the work carefully, which they did in this way: they washed the fish and placed it in the vessel with water, at the side of the fire, putting in [the fire] various stones, and as soon as they were fully heated, they threw them in the vessel, thus boiling the water, and maintaining it in this state until the fish was cooked to their liking. They returned the stones to the fire as soon as it was perceived that they [had cooled and] were not assisting, and changed them for others, making use of a sort of tongs made from a stick broken in half. After having seen this operation we returned to the ships well satisfied with Macuina, and on our arrival various canoes came out, which were going to fish, confirming [that] the weather was well settled.[5]

Another benefit we gained from this putting back to Nutca was to disembark a sick Marine and replace him with a seaman gunner who was an excellent hunter. Also, we asked for the leech from the *Aránzazu*, Luis Galvez,[6] in whose competence the crew had great confidence, and transferred the leech of *Sutil* to *Mexicana*, which was short one man from its complement of twenty four, with which it had been decided the goletas should proceed with the exploration.

At two thirty in the morning [of June 5th] the boats were ordered, and at three we were outside the points. The wind was

---

[4] This word is in AGN Hist 558, but not in MN 619.

[5] This paragraph, except for part of the last sentence, is omitted from the *Viage*.

[6] The only crew member named in the narrative.

light from the NNW, the weather fair, and appeared sufficiently
settled to enable us to lay a course to pass near the shoals of the
Punta de Arrecifes. The wind dropped as soon as we left the
inlet which formed the entrance to Nutca, and a near calm
followed until eleven in the morning, when it set in from
WSW. It freshened in the afternoon, and we proceeded under
full sail, reaching close to seven knots, the best rate we had
experienced in the goletas. From five until seven the wind held,
and at dusk we were sixteen miles W 10° N from the entry of
Nitinat and five miles from a small islet which was abeam.

Our instructions required us to expedite the exploration of
the entry of Juan de Fuca; for this reason we delayed examining
the parts of the coast which were in view, and only took running
fixes to locate some points and ratify the charts of the coast made
by the officers and pilots of the Department of San Blas, which
were good for detail.

We continued sailing during the night under full sail [on a
course of] E 5° S with a light breeze from the WSW, in the
confidence that the clearness of the night, aided after ten by the
moon, kept us safe. At two in the morning the wind dropped to
a near calm, and in this way we were about half a league to the
southeast of the east point of Nitinat at daylight and in view of
the mouth of the Strait or Entry of Juan de Fuca.

Until eleven it remained calm, and the current carried us
into the strait about a league. We saw a heavy chop caused by the
current, without a corresponding turbulence. As soon as we
approached this, we saw on the north coast, about half a league
off, blades of seaweed which sailors know under the name of
sargaso.[7] We took a sounding in the choppy water and found 32
fathoms of depth. The mariner accustomed to sailing close to
coasts is aware that this seaweed is often a sign of shallow water,
as is at most times the chop, formed by the currents meeting an

---

[7] In all likelihood kelp, which translation is used hereinafter.

obstacle in their path; we had confirmed this on various occasions in our own experience.

At eleven o'clock the southwest wind came up and we pointed the prow ESE to cross the mouth of the strait.[8] At four in the afternoon the Puerto de Núñez Gaona was sighted, and soon after a corvette at its anchorage, which we surmised to be *Princesa*, belonging to the Department of San Blas. We set a course to close the west part of the port, and soon Ship Lieutenant Don Salvador Fidalgo, commandant of *Princesa*, arrived. He confirmed our notion that the west shore of the port was foul ground, as indicated by the kelp. This left us with little sea room, but at the cost of several tacks we succeeded in anchoring at six thirty in the evening very close to *Princesa*.

---

[8] The *Viage* here reports a meeting with some Indians, who traded a big fish for a knife.

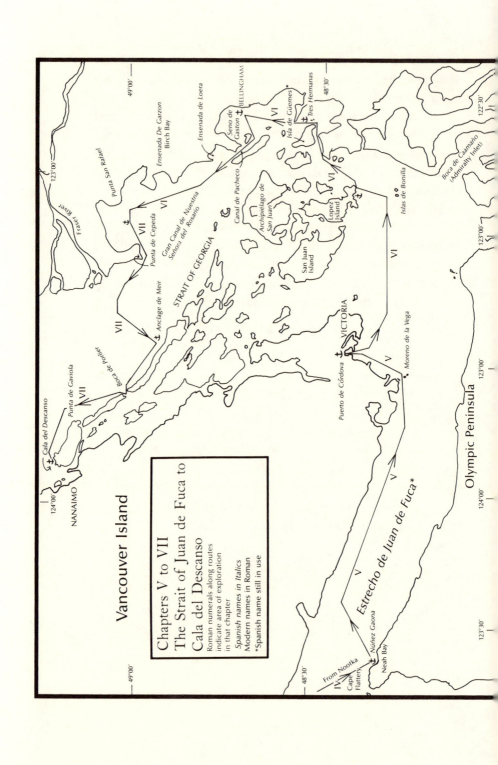

Vancouver Island

Chapters V to VII
The Strait of Juan de Fuca to
Cala del Descanso

Roman numerals along routes
indicate area of exploration
in that chapter

Spanish names in Italics
Modern names in Roman
*Spanish name still in use

STRAIT OF GEORGIA

NANAIMO

Cala del Descanso

Punta de Gaviola

Boca de Poitier

Anclage de Meir

Punta de Cepeda

*Gran Canal de Nuestria
Señora del Rosario*

Punta San Rafael

Fraser River

Ensenada De Garzon
Birch Bay

Ensenada de Loera

*Seno de
Gaston*
BELLINGHAM

Isla de Güemes

Tres Hermanas

Canal de Pacheco

*Archipiélago de
San Juan*

San Juan
Island

Lopez
Island

Islas de Bonilla

Boca de Caamaño
(Admiralty Inlet)

VICTORIA

Puerto de Córdova

Moreno de la Vega

*Estrecho de Juan de Fuca**

Núñez Gaona
Neah Bay

From Nootka
Cape
Flattery

Olympic Peninsula

49°00'

48°30'

48°30'

49°00'

124°00'

123°00'

122°30'

123°00'

123°00'

124°00'

123°30'

123°30'

V

The Commandant of Princesa *prepares to form an establishment at Núñez Gaona on the model of Nutca: An idea of the terrain and port: Good harmony with the Indians: No difference in their customs to the Nutcas: Precautions of Fidalgo to avoid untoward occurrences: The chiefs Taissoun and Tetacus visit the goletas: Observations at Núñez Gaona: Tetacus accepts an invitation to make his voyage into the Strait in the goletas: The part explored by the officers Quimper and Elisa, and the plan of our operations: The goletas leave Núñez Gaona: The preferred track to sail into the Strait: Friendly warnings of Tetacus: The goletas arrive at the Puerto de Córdova: Anxiety of Tetacus until the canoe arrives with his wife María: Visit to the natives: Character of Tetacus: Words in the language of Fuca.*

It had been a month[1] since the arrival from San Blas of the corvette *Princesa*, and its commandant, Fidalgo, was awaiting orders from Commandant Quadra, either for the formation of an establishment, or the abandonment of the harbour. [Quadra had] to negotiate this matter with the English commissioners who were expected at Nutca[2] to finalize the convention made between our Court and that of England in 1789. Fidalgo had selected and cleared a site for a garden, starting to set out nursery plants he had brought from San Blas in containers. He had built an enclosure for raising livestock, which consisted of cows, sheep, hogs, and goats. He had also built a stockade close by, where a guard of soldiers was maintained to provide custody and good order. Fidalgo had put this work in hand to prepare

---

[1] More like a week. *Princesa* arrived on May 28th. AGN Hist. 67.

[2] George Vancouver, who was in fact inside the Strait of Juan de Fuca at the time.

for wintering [at the site] if the establishment was decided on.[3]

Although the soil is of the same type as that at Nutca for cultivation and crops, it appears more fertile, and the climate more pleasant and healthy. The country is watered by small streams, and sheltered by well placed mountains. The harbour is exposed to northwest winds, and even winds from a generally southwest direction blow in violently, constricted by a gorge through the mountains in this direction. Rocks extend some distance from the beaches, and the surf breaks on them, making it difficult and risky to disembark.

The Indians were most friendly, [having been] honoured by Fidalgo and given presents in the same way as those of Nutca [had been honoured] by Quadra. Although their language is very different,[4] the islanders and their customs appear to be the same. During our stay we found them affable, trusting, and quick-witted, sturdier than those at Nutca, and the women of more pleasing appearance. The clothing of [the women] was not modest; they go nude with a skin fastened at the neck, without other covering except for some grass fringes suspended from a cord attached to the belt, sufficient to cover the private parts, in the way of the Indians of California. They expose themselves without embarrassment and with very little modesty in their canoes and ashore. They go around [with the arms] covered with copper or carved deer antler bracelets, and with necklaces of shells, whalebone, copper, or beads. The pendants [hanging] from their ears and from their noses, of which the cartilage is also pierced, are decorated in the same way. They paint themselves red and black, using grease to make their hair shine, and they know how to take more care of their extravagant [adornments] than the women of Nutca.

They have little appreciation for Monterey shells[5] or iron;

---

[3] Here are found many deletions and amendments, the latter in another hand. The original, which corresponds with AGN Hist. 558, has been followed.

[4] The notes in MS 330 say that the languages are similar.

[5] Abalone, valued as decorative material elsewhere on the coast.

even copper is not held in particular esteem. Used clothing is the currency most employed among them. However, here as with the rest of these savages, they have only been seen to put on any cloak or coat at the time of exchange if they can soon manage it well. We did not see that they had an abundance of peltries or other objects of exchange. Some ordinary coats, spun and woven from the hair of sea otter skins and wool of dogs shorn for this purpose, were only of interest as curiosities. The wool of these animals is very fine, and according to the [zoological] system of the Count of Buffon[6] they are indigenous to America. Their barking is limited to a mournful howl.[7]

Fidalgo did not place much faith in the natives, intending thus to avoid any fatal accident, knowing that there had been attacks by these Indians on ships which had appeared on this coast. Accordingly, he had caused a cannon to be fired at sunset, which signal he had made them understand to mean that from then until dawn, they should not approach the ship or our shore establishment. He soon found them to observe this point of discipline with the greatest docility. For the same reason he had not wished to give them arms, and even though they asked us, we would not give them knives.

One of their chiefs,[8] Taissoun came alongside soon after we anchored, and gave us some sardines before coming aboard. This was an action we had never seen in Nutca, nor could we expect it, considering the poverty and the needs of these savages. We reciprocated with shells, beads, and some ship's biscuit. He looked around the ship and withdrew well satisfied with our treatment.

Tetacus, who was one of the principal chiefs, and by his conduct together with later information, one of the most devoted to the Spaniards, also came aboard and asked with the greatest

---

[6] French naturalist and writer, 1707-88, whose "Histoire Naturelle" was a standard work.

[7] The *Viage* adds a paragaph, taken from the MS 330 notes, saying that only chiefs were admitted aboard, and that women were offered to the visitors by a youth.

[8] The word "Gefe" is used here, rather than "tais" and has been translated.

politeness for permission to look over the ships. This was given him, and he examined them with a curiosity we had not seen in any of these savages. Afterwards he told us that one of those waiting alongside was his wife, whom he called María, a name which could have seemed to be a corruption of pronunciation, if we had not listened with care to that of Tetacus. With this news, we instantly pressed her to come aboard. She excused herself with an air of embarrassment and hesitation. We assured Tetacus that we had no other purpose in asking her aboard than respect for her, and that if she wished to accept, she could be assured that she would not receive the slightest insult or incivility. Her husband then ordered her to come, and she obeyed, stretching out her hand by which we assisted her. They were highly pleased. We presented some trifles to them, and they went, leaving us fully content to see that this Indian chief had the necessary feeling of freedom and confidence to be with his favourite wife alone and unarmed on a ship he had just seen, and whose crew had not even given evidence on which to form a good impression.

Our operations and observations in this port were limited to making a plan of it, observing its latitude with the sextant by obtuse or back angles of the sun[9] and [observing] the longitude by the chronometers. The thermometer stood at 16 to 19 degrees.[10] The eudiometer gave the following results which proved the superiority of the healthiness of the air to that at Nutca.

Open air	65 parts
Repeated	67
Air in the depth of the forest	63
Air in the pigsty built on the ground	53
Repeated	53

At the time the wind was slight, and the thermometer at 19 degrees.

---

[9] Land lay to the south, so it was necessary to measure the angle of the sun with the northern horizon.

[10] 20 to 24 degrees Celsius.

The weather had remained beautiful, and on the 8th [of June] we were ready to set sail, having received from Fidalgo a pit saw, some tallow, and medicines. We awaited only the arrival of a steady wind to set sail. At eight in the morning Tetacus came to the *Mexicana*, and gave us to understand that he also intended to go into the Strait. He was urged by Valdés to accompany us, and quickly accepted the offer. He sent away the canoe in which he had come, keeping a small portion of fish and whale for provisions during the voyage. Soon a large canoe came with his wife María, accompanied by others, and their tender expressions and entreaties made the Indian chief hesitant to accompany us, but when we redoubled our urging he sent his wife away in the canoe to make the voyage into the Strait.[11]

Ship Ensign Don Manuel Quimper had explored this Strait as far as the Puerto de Quadra in 1790 in the sloop *Princesa Real*, and Ship Lieutenant Don Francisco de Elisa had sailed from Nutca in 1791 with a storeship named *San Carlos* and a schooner named *Saturnina*, and had advanced the explorations as far as the large Canal de Nuestra Señora del Rosario. They had examined all the bays and entries but not the Boca de Caamaño and Boca de Flon, Seno de Gaston, the Canal de Floridablanca,[12] and the Bocas of Carmelo and Moñino.[13] By the information we had acquired from the Indians, Caamaño was very long, but its depth did not permit anything but a canoe to pass, while Flon was of very little consequence.[14] They left some doubt as to whether the Seno de Gaston was closed, and similar doubt about the most interesting exploration, the Canal de Floridablanca. According to the chart we had of the Strait it had two entrances formed by an island in its mouth, which after our examination was [shown to be] the peninsula terminated by the points of Cepeda and Lángara. The inlet, as we understood

---

[11] The *Viage* varies and expands this account.

[12] A non-existent inlet thought to be where the estuary of the Fraser River lies.

[13] The *Viage* calls this inlet Mazarredo, a name which appears only on later maps.

[14] These inlets are the entrances to Puget Sound, which both Eliza and Galiano dismissed as of no consequence.

the Indians, was very long. These Indians, who were from that place, had some copper bracelets engraved with a very good design, which they had found.

With this information, we decided to go inside to finish the examination of the Seno de Gaston, and to proceed to the Canal de Floridablanca, leaving those of Caamaño and Flon, being of less substance, and more suitable to check in the probable case that we should return. The direction of the Canal de Caamaño was towards the south, and the probability was that it would lead to the entry of Ezeta, at approximately 46° 15′ of latitude. This consideration helped in our preferring our plan. [15]

At noon the wind came in from the southeast. The clear weather indicated to us that the westerly would prevail in the inlet. At twelve thirty we set sail and steered to pass through the small channel lying to the east of the islet in the entry, which we attained easily. This channel is much restricted by shoals, [which lie] off the points which border it, and thus it should only be used when necessary or for a decided advantage. It appeared to us to advance the voyage, since we intended to follow the south shore of the Strait. Good anchorages were as plentiful on the south as on the north shore. The terrain is mountainous, but to the north the mountains are lower and broken, presenting agreeable views in places, covered with grass and low pines, [16] and to the appearance, good for sowing. [17] In contrast, those of the south side are very high, and their summits are covered with snow. As soon as we got into the inlet, we recognized that the only course to adopt was to close the north shore. Along the route we had intended to follow, a perfect calm prevailed. When we saw a ripple from the wind in the inlet, it was necessary to launch the boat and man the oars to

---

[15] The narrative was edited in Mexico after the voyage, at which time Galiano knew the extent of Puget Sound from Vancouver's map. The preceding paragraphs were probably written to justify his decision not to explore it.

[16] Pino; a word used as a generic term for coniferous trees by both Galiano and Vancouver.

[17] Galiano must have been misled by distance. The mountains in the southwest part of Vancouver Island are heavily forested.

get to the wind. The need for this was confirmed by Tetacus, who was in *Mexicana*, since although on leaving port he did not wish to go, he yielded on reflecting that if his wife and people saw us [without him] they would believe we had killed him, and to us it appeared opportune to oblige him to come, to answer his people and give assurances of our friendship and good treatment.[18]

As soon as we reached the wind, we made for the north side, sailing NNE and falling off to the east when our course brought us close to land. At eleven at night we laid a course parallel to the shore, at a distance of slightly less than a league, and sailed on a fresh northwest wind on a clear and beautiful night.

Dawn [on June 9th] found us close to the point of Moreno de la Vega, and we luffed to pass between it and the islets in whose proximity lay a route indicated by Tetacus, which had been recommended by what we had heard of the strait. This having taken place, we continued with light breezes from the west to south all morning. A number of small canoes came out from the shore, close to the point of Moreno de la Vega, and we gave beads to the Indians in three canoes which came alongside. The Indians understood the language of the Nutcas, and one of our sailors knew one of the Indians, who in the previous year had been one of those most deeply involved in taking the launch of the storeship *San Carlos*. We steered for the Puerto de Córdova where Tetacus indicated he would leave us, having slept peacefully during the night, never setting aside his friendliness and trust. He gave continuous proof of his clear intelligence and understanding, asking about the use of all the equipment. He recognized on the map the configuration of the Strait and the islands we had come across, and told us the names they had given them. When we had turned the point of Moreno de la Vega he advised us to take on water, which was good and plentiful, and said that farther on springs were scarce, and the

---

[18] The *Viage* adds a presumed invocation for wind by Tetacus, not based on the notes in MS 330.

water bad tasting. He ate freely of whatever was given to him, in everything imitating our actions, which he was always observing carefully. He knew the names of all the English and Spanish captains who had visited the coast of the mainland or the Archipiélago de Claucuad and Nutca, and even told us there were two ships inside the Strait.[19]

At eleven in the morning we made the Puerto de Córdova, and anchored in six fathoms sand in the deep that lay in the south [part of the harbour.] The canoe of Tetacus's wife had not yet arrived, and he was most disturbed. He took the telescope and searched all parts of the horizon, showing by all his words and actions that he had the most tender affection for María. This continued until nearly one in the afternoon, when the canoe arrived. In it came also the other wife who appeared to have an extreme love for Tetacus from the emotions she showed in Núñez Gaona, and from those she showed on seeing him. He got into the canoes, [sic] embraced them, and returned on board, where he ate with us. This time our invitations did not prevail on either of his wives to come aboard, doubtless because of the distrust of the old one who could not overcome either her fear of her diminished strength or the weakness of her spirit. Afterwards, Tetacus went ashore with his wives, taking among other presents a waterproof woollen cloak and a hat belonging to Valdés, which he had worn on the voyage.

We noticed that the canoe carried on its prow a large eagle carving, and found out that eagle feathers were held in particular esteem among them. We understood that in this way, like the Indians of the Presidios, they have the tradition that this bird pulled one of them out of a well, for which beneficence they maintained due gratitude to it.[20]

In the evening we were ashore visiting the villages of Tetacus in which there were some fifty Indians. They offered cloaks for

---

[19] The *Viage* here describes another meeting with Indians in canoes.

[20] A legend of a bird with horns which could seize a whale and fly away with it is here added in the *Viage*. The legendary thunderbird is usually depicted with horns.

Gefe de la entrada de Juan de Fuca.
Cetacus.

Tetacus, the chief who sailed through the Strait of Juan de Fuca in *Mexicana*, while his two wives, shown below, followed in a canoe.

Courtesy of Museo de América, Madrid.

Muger de Fetacu Atanaü de Fuca.

Segunda Muger de Fetakü.

us to sit on, bringing out a helping of octopus, which was all they had, and all gathered around us. Tetacus acknowledged the kindness and friendship of his hosts,[21] alternating his expressions with continuous embraces. They gave us as many courtesies as were within their capability, and we retired aboard very satisfied. In the night the port was completely quiet, and we kept the watch required to avoid an unfortunate incident, since although well assured of the friendship of Tetacus, we did not then know the degree of respect and submission of his people. Afterwards, we learned that he is one of the leaders most feared on this coast, and that he had achieved their respect and authority by his bravery. His intelligence and cleverness showed an uncommon grandeur of soul, and the action of trusting himself to travel in the goletas with the few proofs of friendship he could gain in the short time we had traded, is no small proof of this.

The words we could verify of the language of Fuca are those which follow, sufficient to show its difference to that of Nutca.[22]

Abalone shell	Guinda	Sail of a ship	Glisapic
Bird	Ucutap	Sky	Taguishamach
To cut	Licitle	Smoke	Cluisac
Ear	Pipi	Stars	Taguisamach
To hear	Dados	To sting	Zujucitle
Land, flat	Sisabache	Sun	Daquia
Land, sown	Guismut	Sunset	Upat-daquia
Mast	Claquesum	To swim	Suishuc
Moon	Stajuashashitle	Tongue	Lacuec
Mountains	Sovachas	I do not understand:	
North	Tuishi		Aya mas
Northeast	Cuasini	Water	Shaac
Rope	Zumocuanelo	To weep	Clejacle
There	Alu	West	Balegsti

[21] Huespedes. This could mean either hosts or guests. The context suggests the former.

[22] Words in the vocabulary which follows have no apparent relationship to Mowachaht, the language of "Nutca," or to Coast Salish, the language spoken to the east of Núñez Gaona. Sources are Chief Maquinna [Mowachaht] and Mr. Baker of the language department of the Squamish Indian Band. The Viage adds place names and transposes some of the meanings.

VI

The harbour of Córdova is beautiful and offers good shelter to navigators, but as far as we could see, and as Tetacus informed us, water is not abundant. The terrain is very uneven and of little height, and as evidenced in the vicinity [of the shore] the depth of the soil over the rock is small. The forest is thick, and the vegetation the same as at Nutca, but with wild roses in more abundance. Some gulls, ducks, kingfishers, and other small birds were also seen, no species other than those at Nutca being visible. It is noteworthy that we saw waterfowl only near the land, and not out in the inlet. It was in this harbour that the schooner *Saturnina*, of the previous year's expedition, opened fire with its cannon on the canoes of these inhabitants in order to defend the launch of the storeship *San Carlos* which came into their preserve, and which they stubbornly tried to seize. In the short time we were in [the harbour] the weather was temperate, with the thermometer remaining between 15 and 17 degrees Reamur.[1]

Since the weather had been favourable during the day for us to determine the latitude and longitude of the harbour, we weighed anchor at three in the morning [of June 10th] on the outgoing tide, which had been flowing in from the time we anchored until ten o'clock at night, and which had raised the water level by eight or ten pies.[2] We were in a near calm, but we counted on the help of the oars and a breath of wind from the north to take us clear of the harbour, and to catch the thermal breeze, which had delayed our entry into the harbour. On our departure four canoes came alongside, which had come from Núñez Gaona, and we traded two hats with their chiefs. One was Totus, who is one of the three principal chiefs at Núñez Gaona.[3] From eight in the morning we started to enjoy a fair SSW wind, which gradually became a fresh WSW wind. To start with we stemmed the tide along the coast, but later it favoured us and we made for the middle of the inlet to get the full force of the wind and to look for the Islas de Bonilla, which are a good mark for the course. We passed several areas of choppy seas, caused more by the clash between currents of different directions than by their strength. We did not find any that drove us off our course to any great extent. At ten we sighted the Islas de Bonilla. We steered towards them and being about two miles away, we left them at this distance to starboard. At five in the afternoon the wind started to die and we tried to come abreast of the southeast point of the Isla de San Juan[4] to come to anchor to the east of it, which we succeeded in doing at nine in the evening, with the aid of the oars, since the wind fell completely calm when we passed the point.

---

[1] Sic, for "Reaumur," equivalent to 19 to 21 degrees Celsius.

[2] 2 to 3 metres.

[3] The *Viage* makes no reference to this meeting or to Totus.

[4] This would have been the southeast point of Lopez Island, one of the present day San Juan Islands.

As soon as we anchored, the launch was sent ashore to observe the emergence of the first satellite of Jupiter, taking along two soldiers with muskets, with the crew of the launch armed as a precaution.[5] We succeeded in making this observation with all the required confidence to depend on it for all the longitudes of the coast from Nutca to Fuca, and we returned on board without having seen even any indication of an inhabitant.

We anchored at slack water, and continued to measure the strength of the current with the log line during the night. It never exceeded one and one half knots. It flowed to the SSE until three thirty [in the morning of June 11th] and at that time changed to the flood. At six in the morning, three Indians came in a canoe, two youths paddling at the stern and bow, and an old man seated in the middle. We spoke several words in the Nutca language to them, to which they made no reply, nor did they seem to understand them. The elder showed us some pieces of whale meat as if asking to trade. We gave him a string of beads and he gave us in return a piece of his meat. He watched the task of weighing anchor with much gravity, after which he returned towards the shore with his canoe.[6] It was seven in the morning, and a light wind was felt from the SSE. We set sail on this to make use of the rest of the favourable tide. The sky was cloudy, and much more so the horizon which could hardly be seen at [a distance of] a mile. We sailed close-hauled to cross to the east shore not only to follow it, and not miss the mouth of the Canal de Güemes, which lies between the island of this name and the shore, but also to clear the small islands which are in the middle of the inlet in which we were, and on which the current was setting us rapidly. Accordingly, we left mid channel, sailing tight on the light wind which veered aft. We closed the eastern shore, and sailed past the two Islas de Morro with the help of the thermal breeze which started to make itself felt from the south from eight in the morning, with a clearing sky.

---

[5] The *Viage* adds the result of this observation, which placed Nootka at 120° 26′ of longitude west of Cádiz. This is within 6′ of its correct value of 120° 20′.

[6] This meeting is omitted from the *Viage*.

We arrived at the southwest point of the Canal de Güemes, which we entered, sailing at first in the middle of the narrows to keep clear of the calm along the shore. However, once we were inside the wind took the direction of the channel, and we closed the south shore to get free of the force of the adverse current which continuously checked our progress. This gave us an advantage, since although the wind was weak we made three and one half knots. The sailing was very pleasant, between wooded shores. On the north side, which from the entry has a sandy shore, we saw a village close to the northwest point, which we examined through the telescope, disclosing two large houses. The Indians, running to the beach, boarded a canoe and steered for the goletas, pursuing them with as much skill as the most expert sailor. They confidently came alongside, an old man and four young ones with an agreeable appearance, giving us black-berries from the quantity they brought in shells of three or four pulgadas[7] in diameter, trying to conceal those they did not offer to us. We responded with a metal button for each of them, and they repeated their presents of small portions [of blackberries] to obtain more profit, from a button, a string of beads, or a piece of ship's biscuit. They also gave us dried shellfish of the kind sailors call clams, strung on a cord of tree bark, and other shellfish of different species strung on thin sticks and toasted over a fire. We obtained enough of these items and also a coat of dog's wool lined with feathers, and a tanned deerskin. Mean-while we were following the south shore of the inlet in 5 fathoms, sandy bottom, as far as the southeast point, where we crossed over, steering for the sheer northeast point from which we passed close inshore, to follow the shore of the Isla de Güemes. Passing between it and the Tres Hermanas we made for the Seno de Gaston.

We saw the Indians off after they had left us all their black-berries and shellfish, of which the crew ate freely, [the Indians]

---

[7] 7 to 9 cm.

having behaved themselves with the greatest trust. They had appeared in scarlet paint and, as we understood, made the preparation with red ochre and the juice of blackberries. We could not make them understand the language of Nutca which is unknown to them.[8]

As soon as we rounded the northeast point we were becalmed, and had to take to the oars to make the passage, [since the point] obstructed the light airs from the southwest, which as soon as we passed the islands switched to the west. We then sailed nearly close-hauled on the port tack to clear the Punta de Solano. The heat was a great discomfort; even though the thermometer stood at a temperate level in the shade, placed in the sun it rose to 25 degrees,[9] and would have risen even higher if we had not encountered the southwest breeze.

At five the wind settled in the south, and we set a course to take us into the Seno de Gaston, which had not been completely explored. In order to decide this point, we followed the east shore to make for the end of the bay, and to see if there was [an opening to] any inlet in it. The wind was freshening, and favoured by it we were satisfied by nightfall that there was nothing more than a small river at the end. The shore which closed [the bay] was low land lying between two slopes, and at some distance it appeared to be an inlet. The depth was from 6 to 7 fathoms, rocky bottom, and we had decided to beat to wind-ward to get outside, when we sounded in 5 [fathoms] hard clay, for which [reasons] we preferred to anchor. We counted on the wind dropping during the night as we had seen it do until then. We were in a good situation to let go the anchor and to be able to examine the end of the bay more thoroughly in the morning. We furled all sail; the helmsman reported 4 fathoms of depth, and we let go the anchor, but after veering 30 fathoms of cable, the goleta was in 2 1/2 fathoms.

[8] This paragraph omitted from the *Viage*.
[9] If this is on the Reaumur scale, it is equivalent to 31 degrees Celsius.

Immediately the boat was ordered to sound astern, at the poop and two cables distant, finding 2 fathoms of depth and [also finding] that the anchor had been dropped in three. This mistake by the helmsman[10] placed the goletas in a situation of some concern, in which we passed the night, during all which time the tide continued to fall so that at dawn we were in 1 1/2 fathoms. During the night we constantly saw light to the south and east of the mountain of Carmelo and even at times some bursts of flame, signs which left no doubt that there are volcanoes with strong eruptions in those mountains.

Mexicana had anchored about two cables more to the west, and in half a fathom less depth. The wind, which had blown all night from the SSE fairly freshly had raised a swell and *Mexicana* started to ground at the stern, for which reason they set out a warp with the launch. Riding to it, they went to work to set sail without letting go until the sails filled. During this time, *Sutil* brought the anchor apeak,[11] and found itself in 2 fathoms of water. As the boat was being raised[12] ready to set sail it was observed that *Mexicana* had grounded. The boat was immediately returned outboard and sent to join the task [of freeing *Mexicana*]. The sails were ready to raise as soon as *Sutil* was apeak, but this manoeuvre, which should have been executed easily, suffered a mishap, the anchor being raised before the rigging was ready. Just as we wanted to make use of the rigging *Sutil* grounded in a bare six pies of water.[13] Right away the boat's grapnel was called for, with a light cable. With the help of the boat, which came back from *Mexicana*, an anchor was carried half way along the warp, and in an hour [the ships] were

---

[10] The word "timonel" is used twice, which means a helmsman. It is not clear why he should have been doing the sounding.

[11] "A pique del ancla." This means to shorten cable until the ship is directly over the anchor, ready to break it free of the ground.

[12] The verb used is "meter", which means to lower a boat, but the sentence seems to require the meaning assigned.

[13] What happened is that the yards and tackle had to be used to lower the boat. In consequence there was some delay in getting ready to raise sail. During this interval *Sutil* grounded.

afloat, aided by the appropriate measures customarily carried out in similar cases.[14]

Immediately the ships were made ready to set sail to continue the voyage, and at eight thirty in the morning were already beating to windward on a fresh breeze from the SSE to get outside the Seno de Gaston. They did not make any water in the hold, in spite of having suffered several hard knocks on the bottom.

After a number of tacks the ships doubled the south and west points of the Seno de Gaston at four in the afternoon [of June 12th], and entered the Canal de Pacheco following the middle of the channel, the wind slackening as soon as they entered, and taking the direction [of the channel] as before. After leaving it we saw in the Ensenada de Loera two small boats, one with lugsails and the other with a square sail, which were following the shore towards the north. We soon decided that they must belong to the English ships, which were in the Strait according to the word we had from our friend Tetacus. We held our course, intending to sail all night and reach the Punta de San Rafael by dawn, to reach the Canal de Florida Blanca early in the day and enter it. The examination [of this inlet], as has been said, was one of those [explorations] considered the most important.

Between ten and midnight we crossed the Ensenada de Garzon. Lights we could see inside it showed us that the ships, to which the boats that we had seen belonged, were in that anchorage.

The wind, which stayed fresh all night, caused us to cover the distance to the Punta de San Rafael by one in the morning. We stood off under lowered topsails, and at two in the morning turned in, soon measuring a depth of 7 fathoms. We turned away, but the depth still diminished, to about 5 fathoms sand. In this situation it seemed opportune to let go the anchor to avoid spending the night looking for the way out. Nor was it prudent to continue into the inlet without additional knowledge.

---

[14] The account of this occurrence was altered in detail in the *Viage*.

VII

In the morning the passage is found to be closed: The sighting of the English brig Chatam *and the request of the English commandant Bancouer [Vancouver] to unite the two expeditions: The wind does not permit this:* Chatam *returns: The goletas intend to penetrate the Canal de Florida Blanca by the Punta de Lángara, and the current prevents this: They go to anchor in the anchorage of Mier: They weigh anchor in the morning: Risks run in the Boca de Porlier: They arrive at the Cala del Descanso: Differences of character of the Indians at these two places, as shown by the events which happened.*

As soon as it was daylight [on June 13th] the boat was ordered to sound towards the entry of Florida Blanca, with instructions to return as soon as they encountered shallow water. At five in the morning we set sail, following a little astern of the boat. Our anchorage had been on the line from the Punta de San Rafael to Cepeda[1] in mid-channel, and we had not gone even half a mile on a fresh SSE wind when [the depth] dropped below 3 fathoms, having gradually decreased to this level. We turned to a direction more nearly parallel to the shore, and the depth still decreased. We set course for the Island,[2] and the depth increased to four fathoms, so we reverted to steering for the Canal[3] but soon we were again in 3 fathoms, and advised the boat, which came alongside. The boat crew also confirmed our idea that the

---

[1] Point Roberts.

[2] This probably means Point Roberts. Although it is correctly called a point elsewhere in the MS, the map showed it as an island. There are no other islands in the vicinity.

[3] Presumably Florida Blanca.

Canal de Florida Blanca cannot be entered between the Punta de
Cepeda and the Punta de San Rafael; in addition we did not see
any opening at the end of the bay, only that it terminates in low
land subject to flooding and covered with trees. The boat
reached a depth of hardly one fathom of water, confirming that
the bay had no opening whatsoever at its end.[4]

The map made in the previous year gave, as said, two entries
to the Canal de Florida Blanca, that which we had just found to
be closed, and the other to the north of the Punta de Lángara.
Our imagination had been so coloured by the configuration on
the map, and by the word we had received of the expedition of
the previous year, that we could not shake off the belief that [the
inlet] reached far into the continent, and thus our thoughts soon
turned to making for the said northern entry.

We tacked in order to weather the Punta de Cepeda, when at
seven in the morning we sighted a square rigged vessel which
came from the location where we believed the ships to have been
anchored. Soon afterwards, we noted that it carried an English
ensign, to which we responded with ours. It continued to close
with us, and we recognized it as a brig. Arrived at the poop of
Sutil, and after having spoken us, a request was made with the
greatest politeness that they might man their boat, which was
trailing astern. We accepted this, stating the pleasure it would
give us, and an officer came to visit us. We continued the board[5]
along the shore, which informed us of the small depth close to
it.

The brig was called *Chatham*, its commandant Lieutenant
Guillermo Roberto Broughton [sic] of the Royal English Navy.
It had come as consort to the corvette *Discovery* [sic] under the
orders of Captain Jorge Vancouver, having left England on the
1st of April, 1791, to undertake various explorations. They had
called at Nueva Holanda, the Islas de Otaiti and Sandwich, and

---

[4] This laborious description was in all likelihood included because, in the view of the
Viceroy, this was the only possible channel to the Atlantic Ocean.

[5] "Vuelta", one of two possible courses when beating to windward.

after having followed the coast of New California from 45° of latitude up to the entry of Fuca, had entered this strait on the 5th of May, occupying themselves since that time in mapping it. We told him the date of our departure from Acapulco and our arrival at Nutca, and our departure from that harbour, that we left Ship Captain Quadra awaiting the English ships, and that they should go there. The English officer said that his purpose was to offer to us on behalf of Captain Vancouver any help we needed, and invited us to the anchorage in which he was staying, where we would find it easy to take on water, something that was not very common in the strait. We thanked him, and offered him in the same way our facilities, and to join him if the wind permitted. However, the wind was directly against the course to his anchorage, and favoured our continuing further, placing us in a situation of being unable to go and receive his courtesies or to make a proper response.

We told him what was known of navigation in the Strait up to the time of the explorations of the previous year, and that we knew of his anchorage, and the nearby lagoon. We told him the burthen of our ships, their draft, and the names of their commanders, and our objective, which was none other than to explore the inlets and plot exact maps of them. We showed him our chronometer, Arnold 344, and told him we had chronometer 61. The officer said they carried an Arnold chronometer, and one of Kendal, that the brig was of 150 tons, drawing 14 feet and that the corvette was of 350, drawing 15.

After the best proofs of courtesy and trust, the officer returned to his ship, which followed the tack to the west, doubling the point of Cepeda. We continued beating, without being able to attain [Cepeda] until two in the afternoon, coasting along the shore called on the map an island, so as to anchor at the Punta de Lángara, to rest during the night and afterwards enter the Canal de Florida Blanca.

There had been a few scattered clouds during the previous

night which cleared up in the morning, and returned at sunset. The wind remained very moderate, continuing to blow offshore from the land we were coasting, and notwithstanding that we sailed two miles offshore to have enough depth, we were soon in 2 fathoms sand. We stood off until we found 10 fathoms, and resumed our course with little wind. At five in the afternoon we observed ahead a line where the colour of the water changed, being very turbulent between us and the shore. We entered it without finding bottom at 20 fathoms. Within a half mile we could see that the current was rapidly carrying us away from the shore and pushing us west to mid channel. We took to the oars, trying to stem the current, but the efforts of our seamen were futile, already [being] tired from the labours of the previous days. [Since we were] going always more to the west it was decided to cross to the south shore to look for an anchorage where we could pass the night. We placed the prow at right angles to the line between the turbid and clear water with a fair wind from the east, and as soon as we crossed it, we steered directly for the [opposite] shore, where we arrived at nightfall, and continued until we sounded four consecutive times in 15 fathoms sand. We let go the anchor and ordered the boat and launch to sound and to determine the distance we were from the beach, finding it to be three cables,[6] and that the bottom was clear all the way, with 4 fathoms depth to a point where the bowsprit would have touched the shore, and that outside it increased steadily, reaching 20 fathoms within a cable, still sand. We gave this roadstead the name of El Anclage.[7]

The English brig had continued its board to the west for four or five leagues[8] and then altered course to rejoin the corvette. At nightfall it was still in sight, and had again tacked away from the shore.

The wind had dropped completely, but after the middle of

---

[6] A cable was 120 fathoms. This would place the anchorage 600 metres from the beach.

[7] "The Anchorage." This must be the place described as the anchorage of Mier in the chapter heading. Its location is uncertain.

[8] 12 to 15 nautical miles.

the night it settled in the northeast, and gave us some concern. There was then no noticeable current, nor was there all night. The sky remained overcast and it rained a good deal, although never heavily, and in this way the dawn came.

In the morning [of June 15th], the launch left with Vernacci to look for a good anchorage to the west where we could rest, thinking it could be found inside the Boca de Porlier, from which we did not think we were far distant. We surmised, and later verified, that our location was between the two points that lie to the east of this entry, halfway between them.

The wind started to freshen from the NE, and we were concerned about our situation if it should strengthen from this direction.[9] The launch, which had left at four thirty in the morning did not appear, and it was already eight thirty, but soon we sighted it, and it returned alongside without having found an advantageous anchorage in the two leagues it had travelled away from the ship.

The wind not permitting the goletas to cross to the north coast, it was decided to follow [the route of the launch] with them in search of an anchorage, and we set sail at nine in the morning making for the Boca de Porlier, which we reached at midday. We entered without waiting for an examination by the launch, which would have delayed us. What is more, we were not in the habit of sending our small boats away, because of the little force they could carry to keep them out of danger and to defend against an attack. We entered easily, since the ingoing current helped us, although the wind, which had continued fresh all morning from the ENE, fell calm as soon as we got into the shelter of the entry.

As we were entering, an archipelago of low and small islets came into view in two principal inlets, one which led to the east and the other to the west. Right away we resolved to sail against the wind into the first one, to have its help in getting out again if

---

9 Square-rigged ships could make little progress to windward, and could be trapped between two points if the wind blew towards the shore. Being embayed in this way could be dangerous.

necessary, but as soon as we discerned it, there came a squall of so much force from the direction of the Inlet,[10] that we resolved immediately to get outside. It was impossible for us to sail to the east. To go on to the west separated us from our objective. Neither of these channels offered sandy beaches, which are signs of a good anchorage, except for one on the right shore going into the west inlet, but [it was] exposed to the force of the wind and current.[11]

It was not as easy to get out of these inlets as we had figured. The current had attained a force towards the inside that we could not overcome with the moderate wind, against which we had to tack, and [make use of] the oars. It cost much labour, and two hours of continuous rowing to get out of this entry. *Mexicana* achieved this by passing to windward of the islet which is in the entry, very close to the end of the shoal which extends from it, in 4 fathoms rocky bottom, which they could see. *Sutil* was running too much risk in [following] the same [channel] that *Mexicana* had left easily, and preferred to pass between the islet and the shore, in which they also succeeded easily.

In these inlets there are various abandoned villages, and one occupied one, [which is] on the west shore of the entry, and from which five canoes came off, with two old men and nineteen lads, all very robust, well favoured, and of good appearance. They arrived at the goletas and followed them, presenting us with blackberries and shellfish, receiving buttons and beads in payment. We also exchanged some bows and arrows for knife blades. In all this the Indians behaved with the greatest friendship and good faith, paddling their canoes strongly when they had not returned the full value of some of their [purchased] articles, of which they already had the equivalent. They followed us for about two leagues, constantly inviting us to their place, and making signs that we should go there with the goletas.[12]

---

[10] The Strait of Georgia, which they had just left.

[11] The *Viage* varies and expands this account.

[12] The *Viage* says they brought fresh water from their village.

Gefe de la punta de Lángara.

Chiefs of the area wearing completely different costumes. They are not mentioned in the text.

(left) A chief from the Punta de Lángara, first portrait of a resident of today's City of Vancouver.

(below left) A chief from the Cala de Descanso, where the goletas anchored.

(below) A chief of the Boca de Winthuysen, now Nanaimo Harbor.

Courtesy of Museo Naval and Museo de América, Madrid.

Gefe del Puerto del Descanso

Gefe de las Bocas de Wentuisen.

Free from the dangers in which the goletas had found themselves, they followed along the shore, still with the intention of
achieving a good anchorage, sailing on a reach to the Punta de
Gaviola.[13] Not finding one, they continued to the Bocas de
Winthuysen, having a fresh NE wind, the sky having cleared
with the day. They arrived at the east point of the Bocas de
Winthuysen and passed between the point and the islet. When
doubling it, two canoes were seen, which followed along the
coast, watching the goletas, and on their coming abeam, they
approached rather suspiciously. We gave them what tokens we
could of our friendship so that they would approach, and tossed
them some strings of beads, but it was not possible for us to gain
their trust. We followed the coast, still with the objective of
looking for an anchorage, and discovered one at a distance of a
mile from the point. The launch and boat were ordered to
examine it. We followed them, letting go the anchor in 6
fathoms sand, stopping between two points. We called this
anchorage the Cala del Descanso, because we determined to give
the crew some [rest] which they needed by that time. [We also
needed] to take on wood and water, if there was an opportunity,
to repair *Sutil's* boat which was found to be leaking badly, and to
make new spritsails for it in place of the triangular ones it had,
which were not a safe and manageable rig for such a small boat
sent exploring.[14]

When the task of setting out two anchors was completed, we
went ashore in the boat, steering for the beach at the head. We
followed a path into the woods, but soon found eight natives who
made signs to us that we should not proceed, showing much
suspicion. We also saw a number of others running along the
same paths, and we soon guessed that they were going to give
word to the villages where their women and children were. We
obliged them by going back, and once at the beach, we made

---

[13] The point had been named "Gaviota" [seagull] in 1791. Somehow this became mistranscribed as Gaviola; later it became "Gavriola" and is still called Gabriola Island.

[14] The *Viage* adds a sentence of self congratulation.

signs to them to show us where we could obtain fresh water. Immediately two of them offered to guide us, with the greatest trust. They pointed out two trickles of water, in one of which were three huge reservoirs in large basins paved with round stones, reinforcing our idea that water was scarce along these shores, and confirming the advice given by our friend Tetacus. These trickles were on the east shore of the harbour, about two cables beyond the location of the goletas.[15]

On the way, we asked them the direction to the Canales de Carmelo, and they clearly gave us to understand that having returned to the big inlet[16] the Florida Blanca entry continued inland, but we could not understand very well. We named Macuina and Wicananish [sic] and pointed towards the place where they were. We could not draw more information from them, because they did not understand the language of Nutca.

We returned to the beach and found six Indians, who were with our sailors, presenting them with handfuls of cured sardines. We responded with beads and signs of the greatest affection.[17]

The difference of character we found in the natives in quite a short distance is noteworthy, such as that between the entries of Porlier and Winthuysen, the first [natives] confident and affable, the second suspicious and disagreeable, but can not the same difference be seen between neighbouring populations in civilized nations? If in those who live under similar laws, the circumstances of education are enough to change character, is it strange that there are differences between these tribes who appear to be independent, and who do not have much trade among themselves? We had observed that they did not go far from their villages in their canoes if not towards a certain destination.[18] Navigators ought to have this [thought] present [in their minds] so as not to place trust in the savages of the coast

---

[15] Abbreviated in the *Viage*.   [16] Georgia Strait.

[17] This and the preceding paragraph are omitted from the *Viage*. A different ethnography is substituted, not taken from MN MS 330.

[18] Galiano was mistaken; long canoe voyages and extensive trade between coastal Indians, and with the Indians of the interior were well established before the first white men came.

because they have found neighbouring ones to be humane and cordial.

During the night we gave ourselves over to rest, dividing our people into four watches, and posting a sentinel in each goleta, hailing each other at intervals of a quarter of an hour, under whose vigilance all the others could rest.

The night was peaceful. We had given the anchor a long scope, and passed from the poop a light cable with the boat's grapnel of *Sutil* and the large grapnel of *Mexicana*. In this situation we could veer a cable to port or starboard and secure both goletas on either side if the wind called for it.

The 16th [of June] was employed in making sails and spars for the boat, and in taking on wood and some water. At the present season we could make about thirty medium loading barrels of water a day.[19]

The savages did not overcome their suspicions, however much we exerted ourselves to make them understand our peaceful intentions. No invitations or courtesies sufficed to make their chief come aboard, and all the canoes kept together, and came to our side with much fear. In spite of this, they continued to trade undisturbed, purveying fish to us. In the afternoon we noted that when the boat was manned to go ashore, they became alarmed, and moved away from the ship; it could have been because they saw that a musket was going in the boat. As a result, they did not return alongside, except for two canoes which came later with four vicious Indians of the worst aspect, and when the boat turned to move off, they followed it. They carried at the bow a fishing implement of two and a half varas[20] [in length] ending in a two pronged fork. Their use of this is ingenious. They cast it to the depths, the fish come and follow it as it is raised, and on descrying the fish they cast a harpoon, with which they capture them.[21] At nightfall we noticed some natives

---

[19] The *Viage* adds that fair copies of voyage notes were made and expanded into a narrative.

[20] About two metres. The length of a vara differed from one Spanish province to another.

[21] This passage is considerably altered in the *Viage*.

pass in four canoes loaded with house [planks] such as they have
in their villages, which rounded the northeast point of the
harbour. On the morning of the 17th Salamanca went with five
armed men, and an assortment of baubles and beads, with the
intention of going towards [the place] where the Indians had
their villages. [We wanted] to see whether they had abandoned
them, as one could infer from the passing of the loaded canoes
and the howling of the dogs, which had not ceased all night.[22]
[Salamanca was also] to examine the islands and bays to the south
and to make notes and sketches. He was to provide the sailors
with the diversion of the hunt, at the same time giving the
natives an understanding both of the effects of firearms, and the
only use we made of them. This was in case it had alarmed them
to see [the arms] in the boats every time we had to send them
away from the ship's side. [Salamanca] found the frames of the
houses, the remains of the fire and shellfish, and found that they
had entirely moved their home, leaving the dogs, which according to the tribal customs would soon follow them by land.
During the morning, we had seen from on board only one
Indian on the beach, looking carefully at the goletas, without
seeming to be worried by the shooting in the woods. Our men
left at eight thirty in the morning and returned at eleven thirty
without having brought down more than one small bird, even
though they had seen many tracks of large quadrupeds. They
saw only one small house with two Indians, which they did not
approach, having realized [the Indians'] misgivings. Also on
this day we took on some water, and in the afternoon took
bearings, going in the launch to the east of the entry and to the
northwest point of the harbour. In the afternoon a canoe came to
Mexicana, with five men and a lad of eight to ten years. This
canoe came from the end of the bay, where they must have
carried it on their shoulders. They came to trade some coats of a
design more complicated than those we had [seen] until then, in

---

[22] The *Viage* adds a description of the scenery.

good taste and choice of colours. We took one for the King. They were afraid, and drew away every time there was the slightest movement on board, in spite of all our signals of peace and friendship to make them understand that they were mistaken. They afterwards made for *Sutil*, where they could not be induced to come alongside with the same confidence. We could not put down this difference to anything other than their having seen the boat leave for the land with arms. Towards nightfall the canoe returned to the end of the bay. Our total ignorance of their language confused us and made it impossible to gain any understanding of these tribes, perhaps now visited for the first time by Europeans.[23]

On the 18th the boat was beached to overhaul it, the work of watering was continued, and in the afternoon we went in the launch to visit the interior of the entry of Winthuysen. We saw the coves which had been previously seen from the land. The second is more sheltered than Descanso, but [the bottom] not as clear, nor with as good holding ground. We afterwards passed by a channel which trended eastward, and from its direction should have led to the archipelago we had seen from the point preceding the east point of the harbour.[24] In the afternoon three canoes arrived at the side of *Mexicana*. They exchanged bows and arrows for presents of some baubles, and with some trust came alongside. They were very ready to come aboard, although in the end they did not do this, even though a dog which was aboard, and which seemed to be the cause of their fright, was tied up. They went to *Sutil*, still in the greatest distrust of this ship.

The dealings we had with the natives, so short and cautious, made our investigations very scanty, and it can be said that they may be reduced to the little that has been written. The failure to understand the language, which is hard and of difficult pronunciation, was also the cause of our being unable either to gain

---

[23] Nearly all of this passage is omitted from the *Viage*.
[24] Gabriola is meant. Their surmise was correct.

their trust or to advance our explorations. They had no difference in their clothing from the natives at Nutca, manufacturing
coats of sea otter skin and dog wool equal [to those at Nutca] in
the symmetry of weave and design. These tribes, who were
fishermen by preference, kept salmon and sardines apparently
[for food] during the snow, after having cured them and
pressed them to remove all moisture.[25]

---

[25] This paragraph and the ethnographic portion of the preceding one are omitted from the
Viage.

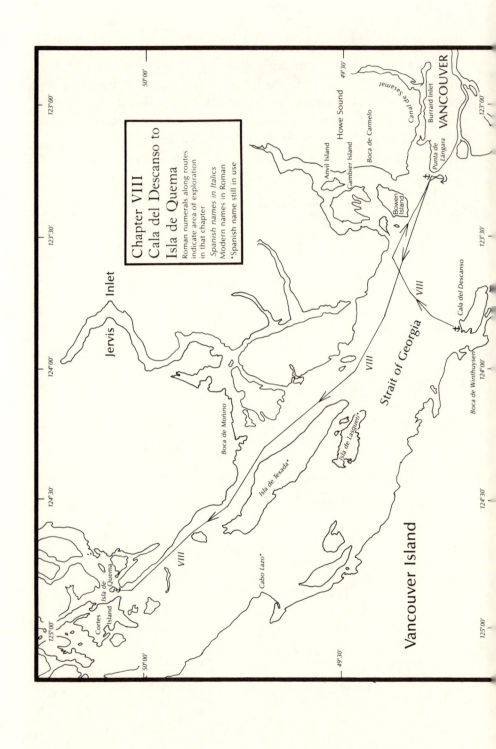

Chapter VIII
Cala del Descanso to
Isla de Quema

Roman numerals along routes
indicate area of exploration
in that chapter

Spanish names in Italics
Modern names in Roman
*Spanish name still in use

Jervis Inlet

Boca de Morino

Isla de Quema

Cortes Island

Isla de Texada*

Isla de Lasqueti*

Cabo Lazo*

Strait of Georgia

Vancouver Island

VIII

VIII

VIII

Howe Sound

Anvil Island

Gambier Island

Bowen Island

Boca de Carmelo

Canal de Sasamat

Burrard Inlet

Punta de
Lángara

VANCOUVER

Cala del Descanso

Boca de Winthuysen

123°00'

123°30'

124°00'

124°30'

125°00'

123°00'

123°30'

124°00'

124°30'

125°00'

50°00'

49°30'

50°00'

49°30'

49°30'

VIII

Canal de Florida Blanca: They cross to the north coast and anchor precipitately because of the shallow depth: They weigh again and place themselves to the east of the point of Lángara: Visit from the natives, and arrangements for the explorations: The English boats come into view, and the joining of the expeditions is reaffirmed: Examination of the Canal de Florida Blanca: The goletas weigh anchor: The English join them and anchor near the Island of Quema.

Not having lost the opportunity to advance our geodetic and astronomic observations for the preparation of the map, the strength of our seamen being restored, and firewood and water replaced, we weighed at five in the morning [of June 19th], intending to go and examine the Canal de Florida Blanca. The weather was clear although with some clouds, and we had from time to time a light wind from astern. As soon as we went into the Inlet we encountered a fresh wind from E 1/4 NE, on which we sailed close hauled, with the bow at N 1/4 NE to cross to the opposite side of the Strait, having a ground swell from ahead and turbulence from the current, although [judging] by the objects on shore the current did not [seem to] have much strength.

While we were crossing the Inlet the wind drew aft; at eight we had already improved our course to NE 1/4 N, at nine to NE 5° E, and at ten to ENE.[1] The wind drew ahead and the sky

---

[1] The wind was veering, so although the goletas had to sail nearly north when they started, they were able gradually to turn towards the east, which they needed to do to cross to the other side.

clouded over. At eleven fifteen we were completely becalmed, by then a mile from the north coast. We were being set onto it, and turned to the outward tack.

At midday, having remained becalmed, and the current going outward, we decided to anchor. We made way under oars to find an anchorage. The beach, which was sandy, appeared suitable for this. We were a mile from the shore and believed we would be in 25 or 30 fathoms, but found no bottom at 60. We approached the shore and at two thirds of a mile from it, we had 60 fathoms mud. The boat was sent shorewards, and at three cables from the shore there was 30 fathoms gravel. Not being able to overcome the current to any noticeable extent with the oars, we had left off rowing until this was determined, and in the said situation were two miles from the west point of the Boca de Carmelo. We made our way with the oars to a half mile from the land, and found 40 fathoms, muddy sand bottom. An anchorage so close to land with so much water was all right in case of need, but not as a matter of choice. The thermal breeze started to turn to the west, and not seeing any great force on the water we steered to the east, and with a light southwest wind we continued until four on a steady wind. We came up to ESE. At eight in the evening the wind built up from the west, and we laid a course for the Punta de Lángara.

From that time we picked up soundings of 40 fathoms. At nine thirty we collided with a log, through a lack of vigilance by the forward lookout. The log got caught up with the starboard anchor and gave us some alarm that we might lose it, and that the log might collide with the boat we were towing astern.[2] The log was a long thick tree, dry, and made visible by its branches. On the 13th we had seen two others at some distance which looked like rocks awash.[3] To confirm in this way that logs were found in these waters, removed any doubt that we had. We believed that these enormous pieces of wood were carried by the

---

[2] The *Viage* transposes this event to a time earlier in the day.
[3] The *Viage* omits this sentence.

waters of the Canal de Florida Blanca, and inferred that it must be [of] considerable [size]. That was the opinion formed from the information we had, and it was our intention to take anchor for the night at the anchorage off the Punta de Lángara,[4] in order to go into the Canal [de Florida Blanca] on the next day.

At ten, being close to low land and not finding bottom at 40 fathoms, it was taken to be imprudent to continue to press the search for the anchorage. We knew from the information we had, and from our own experience, that the depth could change quickly from very great to very little, for which reason we preferred to spend the night standing on and off.[5]

We followed the outward board until two in the morning, when we tacked, steering to the north northwest under topsails. At three thirty [in the morning of June 20th], with daylight, we arrived at the Punta de Lángara. We continued to sound closely, but although at three[6] we found no bottom at 40 fathoms, at three fifteen we suddenly found ourselves in 3 fathoms. We came up into the wind, which was fresh from the west, and seeing that the water was shallowing, we came to anchor in a good two and a half fathoms, on the principle that the sea would set us towards the shore. However, after anchoring it was apparent that the current was setting outwards, for which reason we reset sail, hard on the starboard tack, steering SSW.[7]

In our anchorage, the extremity of the Punta de Lángara bore N 15° W, and the visible extremity of the Punta de Cepeda S 49° E. The Punta de Lángara is high, and [high ground] follows the coast to the southeast for half a mile, but beyond that it is low and swampy with no rising ground until near the Punta de Cepeda.[8] During the previous year this part of the coast had been seen from some distance, and the low ground being out of

[4] This anchorage is shown on the 1791 map, with some soundings.

[5] The preceding two paragraphs are reduced to a few sentences in the *Viage*.

[6] Six in the MS, evidently an error.

[7] The *Viage* records a meeting with seven canoes before the goletas left this anchorage.

[8] This was the estuary of the Fraser River.

sight,[9] they had taken the points of Lángara and Cepeda to be islands, which were at the entry to the great Canal de Florida Blanca.

All the coastline from the Canal de Güemes to the Bocas de Moñino is low lying close to the sea, and behind rise high mountains, whose summits are covered with snow. In the Canal de Florida Blanca there is a wide valley between the mountains, so that at some distance the swampy land is lost [to view] which as said appears like the entrance of a great inlet. The goletas continued on a course of SSW in water deepening progressively to 10 fathoms, but shortly could not find bottom at 60. We held the same tack until seven thirty in the morning, to bring the Punta de Lángara to a bearing of N 3° E. We tacked to the NNW to steer close to it.[10]

At nine we saw four canoes along the southern part of the Punta de Lángara; three were small, carrying three Indians in each. The other was large, and six were in it, including two lads paddling, and an old man of notable dignity, with his cap showing him to be a chief. We greeted them with beads, but they showed signs of holding them in little esteem, and preferred iron or copper. We exchanged two small sheets of this metal of five or six pounds weight for a canoe, which we needed for communication between the goletas, when our boats were sent on some exploration, as we intended to do. The chief came aboard as soon as we made him the offer, in full confidence.

The wind freed to the southwest, and we stayed on our tack until the most northerly part of the Isla de Lángara bore S 85° E,[11] always sounding carefully to be sure there was [enough] water between the shore and the point. We turned away from the wind to find bottom to the east of the point, where we knew

---

[9] Because it was below the visible horizon from the small schooner *Santa Saturnina*, in which Narváez was exploring.

[10] With a westerly wind, Galiano wanted some sea room before making for the point. Even when he tacked, he made for a point well off the Point of Lángara.

[11] In places, the manuscript still refers to Lángara as the "Isla de Lángara." It has been struck out in most cases, but this is one that was missed.

there was a sand bank. There we hoped there would be [enough] water to go up the inlet, as far as the depth would permit. The plan was to send the launch and boat sounding ahead, at [a distance of] about two cables, and to follow with the goletas, not venturing them until the wind was very light. Having noticed that the current at the place where we anchored reached 4 2/3 knots, we had to assume that it would be stronger in the river. The water at our anchorage was almost fresh. We saw heavy logs floating by this place, and all these indications confirmed our opinion that the Canal de Florida Blanca was a major river.

The wind remained nearly calm, advancing us very slowly, and we sounded continuously with 70 fathoms, never touching bottom, until we suddenly hit 25, and immediately 15, after which we manoeuvred to drop anchor, which was done promptly in 10 fathoms. We let the anchor go in that depth, taking a bearing from our anchorage to the northerly part of the Punta de Lángara at E 5° N and to the middle one of the rounded islands which are in the Bocas de Carmelo at N 5° E.

In the afternoon twelve canoes came, and the natives treated us with the greatest friendship and trust. It appeared that they had the same language as those at the Cala del Descanso,[12] but they have a more noble soul and are better disposed. They easily repeated what was said to them. One came aboard; he was saluted and decorated with a ribbon, with which he was very content, giving many embraces to the person who had adorned him. The Malbourg[13] was sung to them, and as soon as they had caught the tune they joined in, continuing by themselves after we had finished. There was some trade of bows, arrows, and clubs, and three paddles for the canoe, since the Indians of the morning went away without wanting to leave paddles for what was offered in exchange. None of them stayed in view during the afternoon, from which we concluded that they were not from the village we saw close to the Punta de Lángara. They had

[12] This would have been Coast Salish.
[13] A folk song about the Duke of Marlborough, still sung in Spain.

made many signs to us that we should go towards the inner part of the inlet, where they invited us, [and where there was] much food and ample water.

After we had anchored we noted that the tide flowed from S 1/4 SW with a strength of half a knot, very contrary to the information we had, but we considered that since we were not directly off the mouth of the inlet, there must be much variation in the currents by [reason of] eddies and backwaters.

At two in the morning [of June 21st] a log was seen coming onto the prow of the ship[14] from which we freed ourselves with the rudder and an oar. The current was never fast, since it did not exceed a rate of two knots. At seven in the morning a boat was sighted, which we did not doubt would be that of the English. It set course to come alongside, and three officers came aboard this ship,[15] being the commandant of the expedition, Mr. Vancouver, his lieutenant Mr. Pujet,[16] and a midshipman [sic]. They told us they had been engaged during the preceding days in exploring various inlets, and showed us the plans, on which we recognized the Canal de Florida Blanca, the [two] entries of Carmelo and that of Moñino. We were much surprised to see that the first of these reached inland only fourteen miles to the east. The second joined together[17] and in a direction N 10° E extended to 49° 38′ of latitude. The third comprised a strait to the east and another wider one to the west.[18] These also joined [and extended] as far as 50° 10′ of latitude in a direction N 25° E for two thirds of the way, and the other third N 10° E. They had also explored the Boca de Caamaño and entered various ramifications [of it] as far as 47° 3′ of latitude, one of these leading towards the north to join the entry of Flon.[19] After seeing our map of the strait, Mr. Van-

---

[14] The manuscript does not say which ship.

[15] Vancouver's journal says it was Galiano's ship.   [16] Puget.

[17] North of Bowen, Gambier and Anvil Islands.

[18] Nelson Island lies between the two entries.

[19] Galiano is describing Vancouver's exploration of Puget Sound.

couver reverted to the undertaking of joining the two expeditions.[20] The advantage which could result in geographical knowledge if all worked to a common end, and the intimate friendly reciprocation of our two courts did not leave us an instant's vacillation in accepting the proposition, which for all reasons ought to reflect accord with the generosity of our sovereigns, whose concerns are to acquire knowledge and present it to the view of all Europe for the advancement of navigation in general, for the advantage of commerce, and for the understanding of natural history, considering the human species as such an important part of it.[21] For ourselves, we would draw the advantage of completing [our work] on this coast earlier, the exploration of the named entries having reduced our interest in them. We could then direct ourselves to the Entrada de Ezeta, and still have enough time to correct the chart to the southward of Fuca.

Under this concept, an offer was made to the English commandant that if his people were tired, ours should go with him if he wished them to convey him. It was signified to him also that the goletas would proceed there if the wind, which was calm, should be favourable, but that whenever they had wind, a course would be set to join his ships, making every effort to respond to his generosity and frankness.

The weather, which continued calm, prevented us from instituting this plan, and in the inactivity in which we found ourselves, it appeared proper to send the launch and boat to visit for ourselves the Canal de Florida Blanca, all the more because no disadvantage could result from this and it would augment the knowledge which we intended to proffer to the English. The order was given to the officers Vernacci and Salamanca to rejoin

---

[20] Vancouver's journal says that the Spanish "expressed much desire, that circumstances might so concur as to admit our respective labours being carried on together."

[21] This effusion has been left intact. The reasons for it are not clear. Relations with the English varied from enmity to alliance and back again during the years after the French Revolution. Galiano may have been covering himself against censure for being too close to the English. The editor of the *Viage* omitted the passage completely.

us in the harbour either where the English were or along the way if they did not find the goletas at this anchorage, since the goletas would set sail as soon as they had a favourable opportunity.

The English boat left for the Puerto de Garzon, and we later saw that the launch joined it.[22]

During the day the Indians remained in the greatest harmony. A crack opened up in the bottom of the canoe we had bought, through which it began to take in much water. It was hauled inboard for repair in the Indian manner, and soon one of the Indians came aboard to direct the work, which was done with safety and a good result. We continued without any new event in the anchorage, without being able to get the feel of the tides, which followed no order in either direction or time.

Although at times we had a southwest wind, it never settled in this direction, and it was usually from the south, falling calm several times. This wind was suitable for the English to manoeuvre to join us, but nevertheless we did not discern them all day. This was attributed to their being busy in taking down their observatory and measuring corresponding altitudes to determine the rate of their chronometers.[23]

The Indians did not gather the next morning, other than one canoe which turned back immediately. In the afternoon four came, with great cordiality. Nevertheless we took particular care, especially at the stern, where they always approached in their canoes, putting their hands into the windows of the cabin. We did not for this [reason] impute them to be thieves, nor because of the missing breeches of one of the sailors. This loss was noticed and the sailor showed his loss by some signs, immediately understood by the Indians. They stood up, taking off their cloaks and [lifting] their mats, and they made it plain that this idea was false. They continued to show the greatest

[22] Presumably the launch of the *Discovery*, Vancouver's ship. His journal says that two boats were used on this exploration; this is the first mention in Galiano's narrative of the other English boat.

[23] This observation consisted of recording the times in the morning and afternoon when the sun was at the same altitude. The mean of these times is a rough measure of noon local time. This and the preceding paragraph are omitted from the *Viage*.

happiness, and we showed the same by all our actions. The Malbourg was sung to them, which they accompanied not only with the tune but also with hand clapping and other motions of their arms and heads. Next they continued with one of their songs, keeping time by rapping their canoes with paddles and other sticks, with an interval of one half second between raps. The song was quite similar to our plainsong. Next followed a different one, repeating the word alesié [sic]. At the end we presented them with beads, and they left after nightfall very content, continuing their songs, and those they had learned of ours, which they took to with great liking, and desire to pronounce them. In the night we heard much shouting ashore. Although we believed this to be the result of their continuing their songs, we did not fail to be vigilant and keep our arms ready.

The non-arrival of the launch and boat, which had left on only a fourteen mile exploration on the previous day, started to give some concern and made us think of setting out to look for them. During the day following [their departure] the wind was light from the north, the tide flowing in this vicinity with little force. The wind went around to the east, from which [direction] it became fresh in the afternoon.

At dawn [on June 23rd], the sky was overcast, with a fair wind from the southeast. The boat and launch were not even in sight, but they came into view at five, and arrived alongside at seven, having examined the east-west inlet which the English had shown us, and adding [to the map] another which leads northward. It had been obscured from the English because of its narrow entry. It ends in a narrow river of fresh water[24] of little depth. Our search reached an end where trees and debris left no passage.

Bottom could not be found at 70 fathoms in the middle of the inlet, and inshore there was 5 to 7 fathoms, rocky bottom. The

[24] Indian River.

shores are steep and rocky, with mountains of a considerable height, with a mantle of tall close spaced conifers, and impenetrable underbrush. Many streams of fresh water, and some cascades, flowed from the melted snow of these mountains, which joined the range to the west that could be seen through the ravines. The mild temperature, the beauty and lushness of the various greens, the multitude of clusters of wild roses, and several meadows with small fruits, blackberries and gooseberries, made it a delightful visit, which anywhere in Europe would combine with brilliance [as a place] for relaxation from work.[25]

Generally the wind followed the direction of the tide in the inlet, not opposing [us] with more than a moderate force, which would permit convenient traffic, without the obstacle of strong currents or whirlpools.[26] From [a time] soon after the boats left the goletas, no Indians presented themselves closer than the outlet of the river of fresh water, in which there were many in villages with their women,[27] who took fright immediately, hiding themselves in the woods. They were given presents and greeted, while at the same time our people were getting ready to avoid surprise, and those who noticed our actions and inferred our ideas left us very quickly.

The goletas, which intended to sail to join the English, to testify to the accord of our intentions, were awaiting only the return of the boats. Upon their successful arrival, the goletas were placed under sail at eight in the morning of the 23rd[28] with the intention of coasting along the inlet, with a wind that was fair from the east, to proceed with all diligence to the union.

At two, a ship came in sight on the horizon to the southeast,

---

[25] The *Viage* expands on this and adds a paragraph extolling the "noble savage," so loved by the philosophers.

[26] An overoptimistic opinion. The tidal currents in the narrows at the entrance to Vancouver Harbour were a serious obstacle to sailing vessels and early steamships.

[27] Probably the Capilano River.

[28] Both MN MS 619 and AGN Hist. 558 give the date as the 25th, but adding up the days in the narrative, this seems to be an error. The date of the twenty third agrees with Vancouver's narrative.

and an hour later another smaller one was sighted. We had no doubt that they were the English ships. They came near as rapidly as if the two ships had been sailing in opposite directions. The corvette[29] came far ahead of the brig.[30] Immediately they arrived abeam, without waiting, we took the initiative to pay compliments to the English commander. Galiano and Valdés went on board them and passed the greater part of the afternoon in courtesies which demonstrated the greatest good faith and trust.

The corvette *Discovery* is a ship fit for the object of its voyage, and even though it is not a pretty ship, nor of good design, the accommodation provided for the officers and crew makes up for these defects, which only gratify vanity and good taste that often run counter to usefulness. It had appeared under plain sail and no more. The brig *Chatam* [sic] is very ill looking, and carried the same sail as the frigate.[31] Both were sheathed with copper and their hulls were very clean.

We passed a good part of the afternoon in the corvette, following the inlet meanwhile under some sail. The goletas did all possible to keep up, and to follow the English ships, which with more sail area continued ahead.

The wind dropped in the evening, and at nightfall switched to the west. We sailed close hauled on the onshore tack towards the north, until we reached it and tacked away, but the wind soon after backing to southwest, we turned to the port tack, easing off. There was some drizzle, with a fresh breeze at times, and although it looked threatening to the southeast, with some squalls, we felt no effects. [The wind] afterwards turned to the south and we followed a course of W 1/4 SW for twelve miles.[32]

The wind continued fair from the south during the night, and at dawn it was nearly calm, but in the morning it came in from the ESE and freshened during the day. We passed the

[29] *Discovery*, Vancouver's ship.   [30] *Chatham*.

[31] Referring to *Discovery*; nomenclature was not rigid.

[32] Altered in the *Viage* to read "W 1/4 SW going two miles by twelve [midnight]."

Boca de Moñino,[33] abandoning the examination of its interior, with the trust merited by good faith.[34] These, like the entries of Carmelo were, as has been said, two arms of the sea of great depth. If we took action to get to know them to the end they would lose all importance. [This was] all the more because our resources were very slight, for which reason we ought not to employ them in explorations of little utility. At the Boca de Porlier, we had been disillusioned by the little way the goletas could make under oars, and made certain that we could not much profit from that place, either with ships or small boats.

All morning we sailed in convoy with the English ships, considerably restraining our progress, but not so much that we could dispute the advantage [of being together]. We continued making fixes to draw the map, facilitated by the clearness of the weather and the fresh wind. At one o'clock the *Discovery* hove to, waiting for Galiano and Valdés, between the two entries of Moñino. The English commandant had invited them to dine. They went on board and were served a meal in the English style, well seasoned. The toasts and courtesies multiplied, and the afternoon passed in this way. The ships followed the inlet with the wind, which although it was dropping, maintained itself all afternoon. Also, the weather, which had begun to look stormy at midday, cleared up.[35]

After passing the channel between the Isla de Texada and the shore, we came upon an archipelago in which night overtook us. The wind had fallen nearly calm, and placed us in a group of small islands, looking for an anchorage and sounding continuously. At last the English frigate found one, and advised the brig of it, which gave us the word. We searched for it with the sounding lead in hand, and came to anchor in 26 fathoms, stony, to the south of an island which we later named Quema because a crew from the *Discovery* set it on fire. *Mexicana* was

---

[33] "Mazzaredo" in the *Viage*.   [34] That is to say because Vancouver had examined it.
[35] All but the first sentence is omitted from the *Viage*.

closer to the land, finding 37 fathoms at hardly half a cable from Sutil, and came to anchor in 28.

Our roadstead was only just good enough to drop the anchor without abandoning ourselves to the current, because it was necessary to make an examination of the various entries which presented themselves, to identify that [land] which was the mainland. We had come across an unknown archipelago, with some high islands, and sharp peaks, with apparently very deep channels.

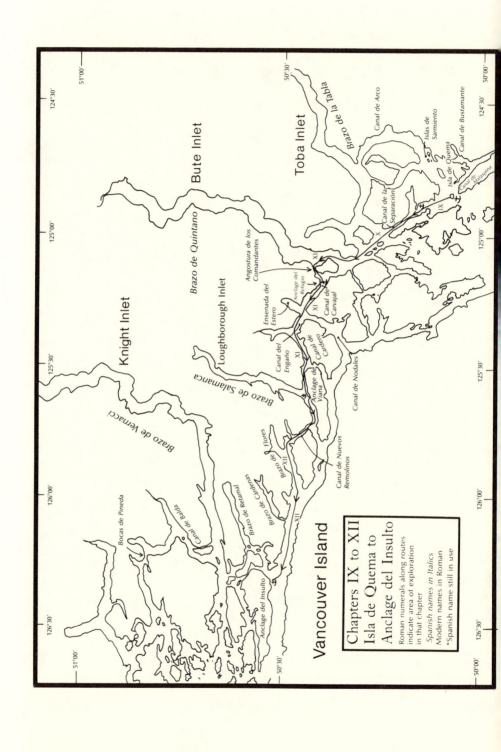

Knight Inlet

Bute Inlet

Toba Inlet

Brazo de Quintano

Loughborough Inlet

Angostura de los Comandantes

Brazo de la Tabla

Canal de Arco

Islas de Sarmiento

Canal de Bustamante

Isla de Quema

Canal de Malaspina

Canal de la Separación

IX

X

XI

Anclage del Refugio

Ensenada del Estero

XI

Canal de Carvajal

Brazo de Salamanca

Canal del Engaño

Canal de Cardero

XI

Anclage de Viana

Canal de Nodales

Canal de Nuevos Remolinos

Brazo de Vernacci

Bocas de Pineda

Canal de Balta

Brazo de Retamal

Brazo de Cárdenas

Brazo de Flores

XII

XII

Anclage del Insulto

Vancouver Island

Chapters IX to XII
Isla de Quema to
Anclage del Insulto

Roman numerals along routes
indicate area of exploration
in that chapter

Spanish names in Italics
Modern names in Roman
*Spanish name still in use

51°00'

124°30'

125°00'

125°30'

126°00'

126°30'

51°00'

50°30'

124°30'

124°00'

125°00'

125°30'

126°00'

126°30'

50°30'

50°00'

50°00'

IX

*Valdés leaves in the launch to examine the Canal de la Tabla and Canal de Arco
and the adjoining entrances: The English do not agree to refrain from examining
the channels that we described as closed: Galiano leaves and examines the mainland [shore] from the Punta de Sarmiento to the Canal de la Tabla: Vernacci
and Salamanca leave and continue this examination to beyond the Canal de los
Comandantes.*

The next day [June 25th] dawned clear. It was agreed that we
would combine our operations with those of the English. Vancouver decided to despatch three expeditions, each of two boats,
to three different channels. We proposed taking charge of one
of these, and consequently Valdés left at nine in the morning
with the *Mexicana's* launch with eight days provisions, taking
the Canal de la Tabla, and took charge of the exploration of
the channels lying to the east of this inlet, giving the English
Commander to understand this, hoping that he would relin-
quish this part [of the exploration]. In this way we would contribute as much as our means permitted to the advancement of
the explorations.

The *Chatham's* boat also left under the command of Mr.
Broughton towards an entry which lay in sight to the northwest,
returning at eleven o'clock with word that there was a better
anchorage in the inlet beyond. At eleven thirty we went to the
southwest point of the Island to observe the latitude, accompanied by Mr. Vancouver, his second lieutenant Mr. Pujet [sic]

and the same midshipman [sic] who accompanied him when we
had the honour of their visit at the anchorage of the Punta de
Lángara. Our observations of the meridian altitude were within
20 seconds.

At three in the afternoon Mr. Vancouver came, bringing the
artificial horizon, and Galiano and Vernacci embarked with the
theodolite[1] and the base of the achromatic [telescope] on which
we mounted the theodolite in order to use it. We had already
made [an observation] with our artificial horizons at the Cala
del Descanso and we wanted to compare their glasses.[2] We were
close to the land at a small beach on the Island when a squall
from the south caused the corvette[3] to drag, obliging Mr.
Vancouver to go back when on the point of taking his observations, and to make for the anchorage found by Mr. Broughton.

Mexicana also started to drag; *Chatham* was sailing under
bare poles, retrieving its anchor, and *Sutil* made sail, under
reefed topsails, because the squall looked bad and we had to pass
by ravines from which some squalls might very well come.

We sailed close-hauled on the southeast wind, which was
backing to the east, until we were close to the coast, and entered
the inlet which was bounded by very high and steep mountains.
About a league inside the entrance the English fell into a near
calm. As soon as we entered the inlet, the wind left us, partly
because of its direction and partly because the squall passed
over.

The English ships being anchored, *Mexicana* went along the
northeast shore and *Sutil* along the southwest, in search of
an anchorage, taking a sounding of thirty five fathoms, rocky
bottom, about a cable from the shore. *Sutil* passed under *Discovery's* poop to cross to the other shore, and the first lieutenant, Mudge, said that towards the southwest shore the water
shallowed. Before turning towards that shore we took a sound-

---

[1] Instrumento circular.

[2] The accuracy of the lenses and mirrors of the different instruments.

[3] Vancouver's ship *Discovery*.

ing of twenty six fathoms, gravel bottom, very close to the beach. We crossed to the other shore, close hauled, but the current flowed with so much force towards the inside[4] that the sails were immediately furled and we resorted to the oars, with which we stemmed the current with a good deal of difficulty, anchoring in the anchorage of La Separación at eight in the evening at about a cable from the shore close to a small beach. In the end, this turned out to be the best place. We anchored in fifteen fathoms, coarse gravel.[5]

The tidal current had a force of one and one half knots, and continued until eleven thirty when it turned to the southeast. Immediately we ordered *Sutil's* boat to the Isla de Quema, with six men, to advise the *Mexicana's* launch of our new anchorage. They were told to make sure to display a pennant by day and a lantern by night. Since this left us without a boat, the canoe being unserviceable after opening up again, a cable was passed from one to the other goleta to keep them together and to move together when necessary.

The night was quiet, the sky cleared , and [on June 27th] the dawn was fair. Although there was a squall, it was not long before it dissipated and left a very good day; Vernacci and Salamanca dined aboard *Discovery* with its Commander, and the Commander of *Chatham*. Desiring to show the greatest civility and courtesy, Mr. Mudge came to take them to Vancouver's ship.

At sunset Valdés returned.[6] He had followed the Canal de la Tabla and inspected the vicinity. [The inlet], which appeared [of] considerable [width] at its beginning, came to an end in a few leagues; its shores were very high, with sharp peaks, its depth great, and the inlets he saw were full of small islands. On its east shore Valdés found a plank,[7] for which he named the

---

[4] i.e. up the inlet.

[5] This and the preceding paragraph largely omitted from the *Viage*.

[6] The *Viage* has Valdés returning the same day he left, apparently as a result of omitting much of the preceding paragraphs.   [7] Tabla

Canal and of which he made a drawing. It was covered with paintings, which were apparently hieroglyphics of the natives. He found some abandoned villages, but not one inhabitant.

On his return from this inlet, Valdés had met the second lieutenant of the *Discovery*, Mr. Puget. He had told Puget that the inlet was closed, but the English officer nonetheless had gone on to examine it for himself. In view of this, Commander Vancouver was informed that the best way of advancing the explorations was to extend reciprocally complete trust, with ourselves contributing the small part afforded by our means, and he was informed that our purpose in agreeing to joining forces had been the idea of working for a [mutual] general knowledge as if we were of the same nation. Mr. Vancouver replied that although he rested his full confidence in our explorations he did not believe himself free of responsibility without doing it all himself, since it was expressly provided in his instructions that he explore all the inlets of the Coast from forty five degrees of latitude to Cook's River. He said that he intended to continue, as he had done from the southerly limit, until he reached the northern one.

From the 28th of June until the 1st of July we employed ourselves in replenishing water and firewood and carrying out geometric [surveying] operations, astronomical observations, and the correction of the chronometers. Winds were very variable in direction and strength. At times the southeast [wind] caused us to drag until we came to anchor in forty fathoms of depth. The tidal currents were very irregular, as much in their direction as in their strength, [both of which] corresponded to those of the wind. When this "southeasted,"[8] the current flowed strongly in its direction, lasting longer than usual, and the opposite [current] lost [strength and duration], being for three to four hours hardly distinguishable. With the same direction of current the water would either rise or fall.[9]

---

[8] Suesteaba.

Our civilities towards the English continued without inter-
ruption. The Commander of *Chatham*[10] invited us to dine and
we responded, inviting the Commanders and English officers
two at a time to each goleta, because the tightness of [the
accommodation in] our ships would not permit otherwise.[11]

The sea was very unresponsive to our fishing, although the
abundance of whales which blew in the Canal[12] ought to have
promised abundance. Neither did the land furnish game, fruit,
or vegetables; we took only a grouse[13] which the people who
were in the boat waiting for Valdés at the Isla de Quema
succeeded in catching. They were able to cook it in the fire
which had broken out on the Island. Although there were many
signs of deer and bear, [game was scarce because it] was so much
harassed by the unseen natives.

The population of the neighbourhood is very small. Hardly
any signs of abandoned villages were seen, which mounds of
empty shells never failed to manifest. In these days only on the
30th [of June] did a canoe present itself with two elderly natives
bringing two quarters of venison. Immediately they had sold
them they went to the northwest part of the inlet, giving no sign
either of mistrust or of curiosity caused by [seeing] the strange
objects capable of arousing it. We were left without having
acquired from them any information beyond that gained from
[observing] the activities and language of Nutca.

On the 1st of July we noticed a piece of the land breaking
away from the mountains and falling into the sea. On examining
the high ground it was apparent that it had been formed by some
explosion of the earth; the part of these mountains that could be
examined was composed of boulders piled without order and
embedded in earth. When this [earth] was stripped away by
rainwater in places the boulders lacked support and fell precip-

---

[9] The *Viage* adds a comment on observing the same phenomenon in the Strait of Magellan.
Galiano had participated in a survey of that strait in 1785-6.

[10] Broughton.

[11] This and the following three paragraphs are omitted from the *Viage*.

[12] The Strait of Georgia.   [13] Gallina de monte.

itately until they encountered an obstacle. Thus many [boul-
ders] were stopped, either on the lower slopes or against tree
trunks. In the southern part of the Canal del Arco which we had
explored, the launch passed below various rocks about a hundred yards [up the slope] on the sawtooth ridge, which were
breaking away and appearing on the point of collapse, and
which would fall as soon as moved by some slight disturbance.
The rocks are of granite and there are few [of other] kinds, even
including the pebbles on the beaches. No volcanoes were
encountered to whose fire could be attributed such a . . .[14]
effect. There were many conifers, some of which would make a
mainmast for a ship,[15] as well as an assortment of species of
plants besides those we had collected, which enabled us to add
to our herbarium during this sojourn.

On the 2nd, the weather was beautiful all day, with a wind
from the northwest until nine in the morning, and then from
the southeast until sundown, switching back to the northwest
somewhat fresher then we usually had. In the afternoon Galiano
left in *Mexicana's* launch with *Sutil's* boat's crew to continue the
explorations, being equipped similarly to the last expedition.

On the morning of the 3rd, hour angles were taken and the
chronometers compared, and soon after the sun set, the emergence of the first satellite of Jupiter was satisfactorily observed,
but the short distance from the sun did not give a reliable result.
The day was fair and the wind fresh, changing from a land to a
sea breeze at the customary times.[16]

On the 4th the weather continued as before without any
increase in the strength of the sun. The crew was the happier for
the killing of a deer which doubtless was drawn by the bleating
of the two goats on the goletas,[17] who had been taken from the
land without their young, which gave strength to their com-
plaints. The ruggedness of the mountains and roughness of the

[14] Word obscured in MS 619, phrase missing in AGN Hist. 558.
[15] Navío: a major ship, approximately a line-of-battle ship in English usage.
[16] This and the next two paragraphs are omitted from the *Viage.*
[17] This is the only reference to livestock aboard the ships.

thickets gives much security to the forest animals, and in spite of the advantages of our means [i.e. firearms] to capture them, the major part of those we had seen dead had been [killed] through the industry of the natives.

The good weather continued, with a fair wind from the northwest during the night and from the southeast during the day. The tide range was one and one half fathoms according to most of the observations made from this anchorage. During the night the launch came back from its task after having scrupulously recorded all the shoreline from the Punta de Sarmiento to the Canal de la Tabla, closely following the mainland shore without omitting an exhaustive exploration of even the smallest entrance. No Indians were met during the whole excursion even though some traces of habitation remained on the beaches examined, including in some places frameworks of village [houses] and quantities of shell which it was known had been heaped up after having contributed to [the Indians'] sustenance. In the easternmost of the Islas de Sarmiento [18] was found also a chest covered with grass. Examination disclosed inside it another [chest] containing [the body of] a child of about two years already decomposed, with his coat of sea otter fur. He had also two necklaces of shells, three fishhooks, a cord, and various articles which apparently had been left with him. If the Indians had done this with the intention that they should be useful to the departed, as is most probable, we could infer [they had] some idea of resurrection. [19]

There was found also a fish trap in a bay which was named for it. [20] [The trap was] made with stakes studded with spines and driven into the sea bed, to trap fish and retrieve them at low tide. This system is well known in Europe in similar circumstances. The finding of these places abandoned at this season proves what we had found, that it is [the season] in which fish are

---

[18] This is a group of islands lying outside Prideaux Haven.

[19] Most of this paragraph and all of the next are omitted from the *Viage*.

[20] "Pesquero."

absent, and that the Indians could not live on the proceeds of hunting game, which is very scarce. In the four days that this journey lasted only one deer was seen at the head of [the Canal de] Bustamante which did not wait to be shot with a musket, entering the woods and frustrating our attempts to find it.

On the 6th Vernacci and Salamanca left in the launch and boat on a fresh southeast wind, to continue the examinations to the west, following the Canal de Quintano with a fresh SE wind, without leaving the mainland shore. In the afternoon of the 8th, being obstructed by a point of land on the west side [of the inlet, which prevented them] from seeing all the shore of the great bay which formed the end of the inlet, they pressed on in spite of the strong undertow created by the fresh wind blowing against the outflow from the streams[21] swollen by meltwater from the snows, in only three pies[22] of depth. On attempting to turn, they could not carry out [this manoeuvre] without the most evident risk of capsizing. In turning, the launch was struck broadside by a sea, being saved by the canvas weathercloths which had been fitted from bow to stern as a protection from rain, but they took the first opportunity to turn the poop towards the sea, and then worked their way towards the part of the shoreline where the confused sea was less and they were able to turn around.[23] The night was spent in a small cove where there was a heavy chop and the wind blew strongly; on the beach were some Indian possessions, notably a chest made like those at Nutca and a net on a wooden hoop with a long wooden handle.

On the morning of the 10th, in good weather, they made for the Angostura de los Comandantes stopping in the large village on the mainland shore. The inhabitants gave them a pleasant greeting, offering fish to them, and warning them not to go into the inlets beyond because there were very strong currents and whirlpools in those channels.

---

[21] Evidently they encountered a tide rip.

[22] 0.8 m.

[23] The last half of this paragraph is an edited version of notes written directly on the sketch made during the boat expedition. It is in MN MS 2456.

The strength of the adverse current obliged them to moor to a point on the Island, waiting to see whether it would change its direction. They sent two of the most active sailors to a lookout on the heights of the island to reconnoitre the bay beyond, who returned saying they did not see an entrance or inlet other than one which appeared to surround the land on which they stood, making it an island.[24] However, the officers knew that there could not be a current of seven knots unless a large volume of water was flowing which could not find another outlet for a great distance other than some narrow nearby channel.[25] They passed several hours hoping for this,[26] until they saw the current was about to slacken. Then, following the example of the Indians, they entered the bay[27] and discovered the entry to the Canal de Carbajal. From appearances it must have been very wide, and the Indians, who by signs indicated their understanding, assured them that it led to the sea.

It was decided to terminate the examination and return by the Canal de Remolinos, but making for the bay the current [at its entry], was already swirling strongly and forming large whirl-pools which surrounded the island. These dragged the launch and boat from one place to another, without their being able to maintain steerage way with the oars, nor could the sail do more in aid of the oars than to expose the boats to a near capsize.[28] After having been unable for some time to make progress, they determined to return by the way they had come, waiting for the moment towards the turn of the tide when the current slackened. They achieved this without difficulty and came aboard [the ships] during the night.

Although the inlet they had just examined was risky because of the large whirlpools, it was decided we would proceed with the goletas to go through it, since the small size of our launch

---

[24] The *Viage* omits this reconnaissance.

[25] They were right; the only nearby channel is the Yuculta Rapids, as restricted as the one they could see.

[26] A change in direction of the tidal current.   [27] Big Bay, west of Stuart Island.

[28] This sentence omitted from the *Viage*.

and boat would not permit long range explorations. The English, provided with good boats with swivel guns to arm them, advanced their explorations with fewer misgivings and less work.

We explained this to the English, and were preparing to separate when on the twelfth an expedition of two English boats returned with word that they had found an exit to the sea in 51° latitude. They gave us a sketch of the plan they had made, on which appeared only one large inlet leading northward and another smaller one. Commander Vancouver advised us of his intention to go back with his ships by the inlet where we were anchored to follow another lying to the southwest. From its direction, it must lead to the one they had just explored, which led to the sea, [the English] having seen the east and west ends of this channel, leaving a few miles between. [Vancouver advised us] that this channel was suitable for his ships, unlike the one we proposed to follow [which was] full of shallows, currents, and whirlpools, making it very dangerous. We confirmed to him our intention of following the latter to continue our explorations.

X

The English ships separate [from the goletas]: The efforts of the goletas to progress are ineffective: The anchorage of the Marías: They meet Indians: Anchorage of Zevallos, of Robredo, of Murfi, and Concha: Good character of the Indians of the Angostura de los Comandantes: Great velocity of the current in the narrows: The goletas pass it, and with equal ease pass the Angostura de Carvajal, and anchor in the Cala del Refugio.

At dawn [on July 13th] the wind was fairly fresh from the fourth quadrant. The English set sail, returning to the southeast part of the inlet. Mr. Vancouver had already sent over his boat, and we sent two maps with him for the commandant of our establishment at Nutca, one that he could send with the Indians if the occasion offered, and the other which he should take in person. Thus we parted after mutual demonstrations of the friendship and harmony which arose from passing a great part of the time together with the greatest cordiality and frankness, which were used to facilitate reciprocally not only a part of the exploration of the channels, but [to share] other geographical knowledge which we possessed, and methods of making use of this. We produced our copies of the maps of the parts explored up to the time of the separation, while the English gave to us a table of positions of the principal points of the coast of New California from forty five degrees to the entry of Fuca, and we gave to the English another table, of various points on the west coast of America, including that of South America.[1]

---

[1] This paragraph much shortened in the *Viage*.

The wind did not permit us to make way against the tide. When it turned to flow inward, at eight in the morning, it forced us to tack several times under full sail. At other times we attempted with little effect to make use of the current in mid channel, or furled [the sails] and put the oars to use, but all our efforts were ineffective. When the tide started to turn against us we had to return to our anchorage, where we stopped in 5 fathoms of water.[2]

At seven in the evening the current ceased, and we made ready to set sail if the wind, which was constant from the northeast, did not get worse, but this is what it did, and was strong and gusty throughout the night.[3]

We had to remain at anchor between one tide and the next, using the time to cut an oar to replace one that the goleta had finally broken, and to secure and caulk the washboard[4] of the boat.[5]

On the 14th, after taking an early observation for time from the beach, we sailed at the turn of the tide, although the wind was constant from the northeast and about as strong. We beat to windward all morning, now from shore to shore, now along one or the other to evade contrary eddies, and to make use of the favourable ones. We could only gain about half a mile to windward, of which we lost about a third on the last two tacks. The tide already having turned against us, we anchored on the northwest side in 25 fathoms sand and gravel. *Mexicana*, which was somewhat to leeward, then wanted to attain our anchorage under oars, but carried by the force of the current, made sail, clawing towards the opposite shore, where it remained about two cables to windward of the place we had left. The wind was steady all day, and abated somewhat during the night.[6]

---

[2] Shortened in the *Viage*.

[3] This and the next paragraph omitted from the *Viage*.

[4] A light plank fixed above the main side planking of a boat to keep out spray and small waves.

[5] This would have been *Sutil's* boat. The boat acquired by *Mexicana* at Nutca is referred to as the launch.

[6] Last two sentences omitted from the *Viage*.

During the morning of the 14th, three Indians came along-side *Mexicana* in a canoe, then left by the inlet to the northwest, whence they had come, after having traded some fish. They gave us to understand that the inlet continued to the northwest until it emerged into the sea, where they had seen ships larger than ours. Their language was altogether unintelligible, but with the language of gestures we could understand what they said, and that they knew of Nutca.[7]

Although on the 15th the weather was similar to that of the previous days, promising no better results whatever forces we wished to use against it, we made sail on the favourable turn of the tide at eight in the morning. We beat to windward all morning, putting in more losing tacks than profitable ones, until at two thirty in the afternoon, having already registered a considerable loss, which dropped us to leeward, we anchored on the southwest shore very close to our first stopping place in this channel, in 15 fathoms gravel.

Mexicana intended at first to make way under oars without losing the shelter of the shore but very soon had to tack, and at the time we anchored, had already resolved, with the experience of three days, not to attempt to leave without a change in conditions, and to continue in the interim the correction of the chronometers.

At nightfall some clouds came up in the northwest, and other thinner ones in the southeast, and very soon the whole sky clouded over, but the wind did not lose its strength or [change] its direction.

Although the 16th was full of omens [of change,] the wind did not alter its force or direction, nor did the ingoing tide have the power to turn the prow, which remained steady towards the inside [of the channel.] This observation confirmed the idea we have expressed, that inside these inlets the tidal current keeps no regularity. The current in the direction of the wind is notice-

---

[7] Paragraph omitted from *Viage*.

able, but the opposite current, restrained by the force of the wind, hardly makes itself felt, and is of short duration. In the night we observed that the southeast current had the strength to turn the ship broadside although the wind was no less strong.

We hoped the day would be more promising than the previous ones, but the current continuing contrary until ten in the morning we were detained. At that time we weighed, continuing under sail until twelve when, the wind having dropped, we furled the sails, preferring the oars and the shelter of the shore. Thus we attained the anchorage of the Islas de las Tres Marías with plenty of work by the crew. Our anchor was dropped in 42 fathoms gravel, and to help it we led a mooring line ashore, leaving the ship secured to both [anchor and line] on the falling tide.[8]

During the night the wind freshened somewhat, and the effects of the increase [in the current] had not been anticipated when the ebb became quite violent in the morning.[9] Azimuths were taken with the theodolite and bearings were established. Latitude was observed ashore and on board by two altitudes.[10]

On the island were wild berries of various species, some fairly ripe and some fully. The land commenced already to look more gentle than in the inlets we had just left. In the morning four Indians came in two canoes. [When] they were at our side they gave us fruit and received beads and other similar presents, leaving immediately towards the northwest.

In the afternoon we took to the oars as on the previous day, making for the other shore, where [we thought] there ought to be more sheltered anchorages. The tide gave us little help, and at times eddies opposed [us with] a considerable strength which the oars overcame with great labour. We came to anchor at nightfall very close to the shore, between it and the Isla de

---

[8] Last sentence omitted in the *Viage*.   [9] Sentence omitted from the *Viage*.

[10] The azimuth observation would establish the variation of the compass. By measuring the altitude of the sun twice, with an interval of time between the observations, latitude could be calculated without waiting for noon.

Cevallos to which we led a mooring line, having anchored in 26 fathoms.

For some time, three canoes had accompanied us, each with three Indians, who came off from a village on the northeast shore. They were determined to make us understand that we should not continue along the inlet, because there were bad Indians who would murder us, and invited us to their lands [instead]. We soon learned that in *Mexicana*, they had been as urgently insistent, constantly showing a generous character and compassion. Such a disinterested consideration and such uprightness commanded all our gratitude.

After having made the necessary observations in the morning [of July 18th], with the favourable turn of the tide at two in the afternoon, we continued under oars in the same way as in the previous days. At first the current carried us along rapidly, but soon we were set back by variable eddies on the southwest shore, and these being for the most part contrary, we had to anchor in the Ensenada de Robredo[11] in 35 fathoms, placing moorings with cables to the land as on the previous days.

We passed the night without wind and at nine in the morning, with a favourable tide, we weighed in search of the pass with the fast currents, which we thought must be quite near, and had the launch manned in order to examine the state of the tide. Finding it adverse we anchored in 16 fathoms in the anchorage of Murfi.[12] Galiano and Valdés embarked [in the launch] in order to examine the inlet, which was called the Angostura de los Comandantes.[13] The extraordinary speed of the currents and the noise [of the water] commanded all our respect; their force surely exceeded twelve knots[14] in view of

---

[11] This anchorage, and several others described in the next few paragraphs, are on the east shore of Stuart Island. Their exact locations are uncertain.

[12] Spelled "Murphy" in the manifest of the Malaspina voyage, in which he was an officer. Location uncertain.

[13] Literally, Narrows of the Commandants.

[14] An overestimate. The actual maximum current in the Arran Rapids is nine knots. The *Viage* gives the current as 7.5 knots along the shore and 12 knots in mid channel.

their violence. The seagulls, which simply alight on the water, go with the current wherever it takes them and take to the air to regain the distance they lose with unusual speed. Thus they maintain themselves, feeding on the sardines which live in abundance in the middle of this current, or on those which escape from the Indians who fish for them in a backwater at the southeast point of the narrows. The Indians make use of a stick with a sort of set of prongs at the tip which take the form of a comb.[15] This fishery is so easy that in an hour they load one of their canoes. When we reached the Indians they received us with the greatest friendship, giving us to understand that we should not expose ourselves in the launch to a passage of this inlet, because we would be submerged inescapably in the whirlpools, as they had been in their canoes, when they had the misfortune to be carried away by the current.

We established that although the current in the narrows was adverse, it was favourable along the shore close to the goletas as far as the same southeast point where the Indians were. The velocity of the current followed the direction of the Canal de Quintano,[16] and the water along the shore flows in to maintain[17] the level lost through the velocity.

We found an anchorage at a distance of a cable along the shore from the said southeast point, which was called Concha, in 15 fathoms gravel, formed as we presumed by the deposits which the velocity of the current must carry to its extremity, and right away we realized that we must be specially alert with the goletas at this anchorage, as the current could be expected to stop. We had to await this opportunity, then instantly undertake the passage.

We returned to the goletas, and carried out this plan, remaining anchored on one anchor in the grip of the eddies, which forcibly changed the direction of the cable, by six points at

---

[15] This sentence is transposed to the previous chapter in the *Viage*.

[16] See Chapter IX for the previous examination of this passage.

[17] Both MS 619 and AGN Hist. 558 use the verb "amanecer", but "mantener" must be meant.

times. The Indians told us by signs that we should make use of the course of the sun, and that at four in the afternoon would be the right time. The view was most agreeable, with the spray, the whirlpools of the current, the gulls, and some logs which passed by, showing the speed of the current by their extraordinarily rough ride.[18]

The Indians left[19] our ships' sides without giving us cause to doubt the generosity of their character, first sealing [their generosity] with unequivocal proof of frankness and trust. For this reason we continued to call them by the name of the good Indians. They presented fresh salmon to us, the first we had seen this year along these shores, and an extraordinary quantity of freshly caught sardines. They let few moments pass without striving to show us the peril in which we were going to involve ourselves, and the time and way to overcome it. They explained to us how to conduct the navigation, and the misfortunes which they had nevertheless suffered, concluding that the mass and strength of our ships would give us not better security than that of their canoes, but rather worse.

From three in the afternoon, the current started to slacken, losing all its effect. At four we observed that effectively the time was right, and we made use of it with all the required activity, accompanied for a short time by our worthy friends who in order not to lose the opportunity to return to their villages soon left us, except for one man and woman, who in their canoe decided to follow us for longer.

In truth, the passage at that time appeared to give little concern, and we had to be careful only to spare no strength to overcome it before the fearful circumstances [of which the Indians had warned] should combine, which would be much worse during the night if we had not come to anchor. We just had to avoid being thrown towards the south part of the shore,

---

[18] Varied in the *Viage*.

[19] From AGN Hist. 558. MS619 says "did not leave", but the context supports the version in the AGN manuscript.

where the launch had observed some whirlpools so violent that they lowered the water level more than a yard,[20] for which [reason] we made every effort to follow the northwest shore on the right. The current propelled us at excessive speed, making the rudder useless, either carrying us towards the north shore or to mid channel, where we would be thrown to the mercy of the whirlpools. Only with the force of the oars, losing a great part of our progress, could we avoid the worst. *Sutil* passed for more than three cables along a stony shoal which lies along the shore at this place, and then the current did not allow *[Sutil]* to attain a small cove where *Mexicana* had anchored. *Mexicana* had done this before undertaking the entry of the second passage in order to look it over in the launch and to discuss whether we should leave it until the following day. The entry had been named the Angostura de Carvajal out of respect for Don Ciriaco Gonzales Carvajal, Judge-Auditor of the Judiciary of Mexico. Out of respect for the officers of Don Alejandro Malaspina he was particularly painstaking in the priority he gave to the Naval Service, and his desire to make the expeditions useful.[21]

However, each time we approached the cove [where *Mexicana* was anchored] we lacked the strength to oppose the force of the current. We resolved to abandon ourselves to the passage, with confidence that the time was opportune according to the Indian man and woman who accompanied us, and who had gone ahead to reconnoitre it. We waited for *Mexicana*, which weighed and followed us, wearing[22] ship repeatedly, [this being] our only recourse to delay somewhat being carried to the inside.

Until then the Indians ventured only to follow us, however much we told them they could sleep on board with all safety and good treatment. They explained that their companions

---

[20] Vara.

[21] A prudent choice of a place name. As an "oidor" of the "audiencia" of Mexico, Carvajal would preside over an audit of the ships' inventories after the voyage. If he was not satisfied, the commanders would have to pay for the shortages personally. AGN Hist. 558 omits the paean to Carvajal; the *Viage* retains it.

[22] Turning away from the wind until the wind is on the opposite side.

would believe they had drowned and by signs exaggerated the drawbacks, at which the woman was the best. We gave them gifts, and the goletas took the entry together with the extraordinary speed of the current, *Sutil* very close to the point of the island. Beyond this, we were carried along out of control, *Mexicana* towards the inlet, where the force of the current was already formidable, and *Sutil* towards the shelter of the point, where it was taken by a strong whirlpool. We were powerless to overcome its momentum, equal to that of a mill-race. We were spun around three times so violently that we were dizzy. Rowing with full strength, we emerged towards the right shore, towards which *Mexicana* steered also, attempting to make it to search for a mooring before night, which was already approaching, and before the current became more powerful than the wind which, constricted by the valleys, added always to the hazards and risks.

The continuous eddies and whirlpools, now favourable, now adverse, and always making steering impossible, held one [goleta] back and advanced the other alternatively, flattering and then mocking our desire to attain a cove which was very close. *Sutil* stretched out a cable with the boat to the east point, but at that moment, caught by another whirlpool it started to revolve at full speed, the jerk of the first turn wresting the cable from the hands which were making it fast. We finally attained the anchorage of Refugio at nine thirty at night, both [ships] under the shelter of a point which broke the wind, riding to anchors in 20 fathoms gravel, with a mooring line ashore.

During the night the wind increased, whistling through the rigging and between the trees of the forest, at the same time as the current in the channel brought a horrible surge with whitecaps appearing, altogether presenting a horrifying situation. What made it fearful was that we did not have a good knowledge of the anchorage we had taken perforce at nightfall.

XI

Continued progress is difficult because of the eddies formed in the water near the Cala del Refugio: This passage is inspected, also the Ensenada de Aliponzoni: Mexicana weighs and makes this anchorage: Sutil encounters eddies, already very strong, which carry it back to Refugio: Sutil easily makes the passage: Mexicana rejoins and they anchor in the anchorage of Tenet: Salamanca leaves to explore the Canal del Engaño, and follows the mainland [coast] to the end of the two shores of the arm bearing his name: The goletas weigh and reach the anchorage of Viana.

On the morning of the 21st the boats traced the continuation of the inlet, and an anchorage suitable for our progress was seen at the Ensenada de Aliponzoni. Watching the tide, it was found that the time for the execution [of this plan] had passed for the day.

Meanwhile the work of replacing the oars of the boats was done ashore, and the crew rested and enjoyed themselves fishing and hunting, in spite of achieving nothing from the latter and very little from the former. We could reckon that all the distance gained from the anchorage of Separación[1] to this point had been by the force of the oars, which because of the heavy task and their willingness to work had greatly tired our crews, as well as their finding no rest because of the discomfort at night. The wind started to get stronger and during the night was squally. The Indians did not appear, nor did we find signs

---

[1] The anchorage where they parted from Vancouver's ships.

that they frequented this place, their misfortunes in these passages having made them so fearful.[2]

Strong wind squalls continued all day on the 22nd, and prevented us from rounding the point to the northwest on the morning tide, to reach the anchorage that had been found. To attain it, the boat had been manned at six thirty in the morning, and in effect found no adverse current. We waited for some lull in the habitual squalls [in order] to make way, but did not get one until seven thirty at which time the tide turned from the northwest to the southeast with a speed like that of a rapid river.

The current which comes from the Angostura de los Comandantes continues through the Angostura de Carvajal, but although it continues in the same direction along the southwest shore past the Isla de las Vueltas at the west end of the narrows, the water flows in two directions beyond some whirlpools, one continuing to the Ensenada de Aliponzoni, the other forming a violent eddy, goes to the Punta de Aliponzoni and flows back to the anchorage at Refugio.

The tide, which we had observed periodically in the Angostura de Carvajal, changed to flow inward at six thirty in the evening. The squalls had not stopped all day, but were not as violent as those of the previous day, and constantly wanting to advance our voyage, even at the cost of some risk, we weighed at seven. *Mexicana* was farther out than *Sutil* and had to undertake the task first. They executed it, and started to gain ground under oars. *Sutil* followed about three cables astern; this short distance was enough for *Mexicana*, although at the cost of some considerable labour, to break out of the head of the eddy while *Sutil*, although almost as well placed, caught it with such speed that they were carried along the bank which forms a shoal[3] along the shore, a cable to the east of the point, at such a short distance [from the shoal] that it was necessary to resort to pushing off from the shore with the oars to keep away. Thus *[Sutil]* was

---

[2] Paragraph omitted from the *Viage*.

[3] The verb used is "arrollar," which seems to be a misspelling of "arrojar" in its maritime sense.

carried, in spite of the force of the oars, [back] to the bay and anchorage of Refugio. A second attempt was made to round the point of the eddy by making for the point of Isla de las Vueltas under oars, catching the whirlpools which carried it to the apex of the eddy so fast that our strength appeared to be powerless to prevent crashing into the shore, but the same eddy carried us back, scraping the shore, to the Cala del Refugio. We returned a third and a fourth time, trying two different ways to round the point, but each time in vain, even though on one attempt we set sail to stem the eddy and get into the current.

When it was eleven at night, and our efforts were useless, we went to the anchorage of Refugio, where we anchored, carrying a cable ashore with the aid of *Mexicana's* launch and *[Sutil's]* boat. *Mexicana* had anchored in the Ensenada de Aliponzoni, and had sent its launch to help us. Notwithstanding this setback to *Sutil*, it was useful to gain a better understanding of the conditions in this passage. During the night there were squalls of wind from the northwest, which *Mexicana* did not have in its anchorage.[4]

On the 23rd, at six in the morning, three canoes came, which we recognized as those of the good Indians we had left at the entrance to the Angostura de los Comandantes. We started the task of weighing the anchor, and continued under oars in a calm, close inshore. We rounded the point at the head of the eddy, gaining that of the Bay of Aliponzoni, and as soon as they came in sight, we signalled *Mexicana* to set sail. The wind was from the north and the current set towards the bay. We countered it with the jib until *Mexicana* rejoined us, close inshore under oars.

Of the three canoes which had come in the morning to visit us, two had followed, the Indians advising us of the place where the goletas should go. On coming in sight of *Mexicana* one of them went to tell them we were following, the other stayed with

---

[4] Last two sentences omitted from the *Viage*.

Sutil, and the Indians, who maintained as much trust as if they were among their best friends, gave us to understand with a pencil and paper, and with books on a bed, the directions of the inlets which led to the sea, and those which were closed.

The current, which we had experienced on the south shore, was not equal to our hopes. Although it was so violent in the Angostura de Carvajal, it afterwards spread out in this bay and its divided strength was reduced so that although eight o'clock was the time of its greatest strength, it happened several times that we could make no progress under oars against the fresh wind, which had turned to the northwest. We had already passed the island in the middle when we found this and started to beat [to windward], gaining much more ground in this way. The Indians, who did not understand this manoeuvre, advised us not to go in that direction, because the Ensenada del Estero to which the prow was pointed, was closed, signalling this with the arms bent and the extended hands one on top of the other. Since we did not accept this, they went ashore on the south side where they made a fire to cook their meal. We continued our tack to the end of the Estero, which we found closed, and turned in search of the narrow Canal del Engaño which continued to the northwest, attaining it in four tacks, but when we were about to enter it the canoe of our Indian pilots came and told us it was closed.[5] The tide was approaching its slack, and we steered in search of an anchorage in the Canal de los Nodales, along the west shore, being already in the period of calm, and anchored in twenty four fathoms gravel in the anchorage of Tenet, a cable from the shore.

The information we had from the Indians did not correspond with that which we had from the English, and thus it was our intention that the boats should explore the Canal del Engaño. Salamanca left in the launch for this purpose at two thirty in the afternoon. Half an hour later we saw the tide begin to flow from

[5] This is a mistake; the channel continues to the northwest.

the north along the other shore, its strength being much less than at our anchorage.

At three the boat left with Valdés and Vernacci, to examine the end of Estero. They rowed all around it and in a ravine found on the east side they saw a small narrow channel with two pies[6] of water, and which diminished even more inside, but which led afterwards to an arm or lagoon which led to the northeast. The shallowness of the bay made this examination of no value. It could be a lagoon formed in a valley by the freshet discharged from the mountains, and its entry was so narrow that it would hardly admit the goletas without grounding. This examination confirmed, the boat returned alongside at nightfall.

The lagoons of the Nuchimases, which we knew to exist by word from the Indians of Nutca, must have been formed by the freshet. It is believed probable that these lands have an extensive interior. In this there is a resemblance to the opposite coast of America which is uninterrupted in all its length.[7]

The calm continued all day. In the afternoon a canoe with two Indians came from the south of our anchorage, and immediately our [Indians] went to investigate it and came with them, indicating that they were their friends. Soon after came another with two women and a child. They steered towards our side, but the Indian men told them not to come alongside. They obeyed at once, but in a little time the men told them they could come aboard. We gave them green beads, which they appreciated, and then they went towards the Canal del Engaño.

At four thirty in the afternoon three canoes came; one large one with five boys, loaded with pine bark,[8] another of medium size similarly loaded with three [Indians], and the third with two in which they brought three salmon. They came from the

---

[6] Half a metre.

[7] Galiano appears to be trying to refute the idea of a passage to the Atlantic.

[8] The word "cascara" is used, literally the rind or peel, rather than "corteza." Remembering that "pino" meant any conifer, it is possible that the load was the inner bark of the red cedar, used extensively for weaving and cordage by the Indians. See Stewart, Hilary, 1984.

Vista del Remate del Canal de Salamanca y sospechoso seguimiento de los Yndios.

The Canal de Salamanca, now Loughborough Inlet
The "suspicious pursuit" of the title is probably exaggerated.
The incident is not included in the narrative.

Courtesy of Museo Naval, Madrid.

entry of the Canal del Engaño, and left by the inlet to the south.[9]

On the 24th there were scattered clouds, and on the 25th it rained, with southerly winds. We occupied these two days in making observations and calculations required for the continuation of the maps, awaiting the arrival of the launch, which returned at night having followed the mainland as far as the shores of the Canal de Salamanca, having arrived at its termination at three thirty in the afternoon of the 24th.

On the 26th, at eight in the morning, and on the favourable turn of the tide, we weighed, and assisted sometimes by the oars and sometimes by the wind, which was from the south, we entered the Canal del Engaño. With the aid of the oars we passed between the island and the south shore, preferring to make our way through this narrow channel rather than the large clear one to the north. The current pushed us along at a good rate, and as soon as the channel took a turn to the WSW, we picked up a wind from ENE, which quickly carried us close to a point across from the Canal de Olavide. There the wind dropped, and left us to go on, aided by the oars, at the will of the current, to the entry of the Canal de Cardero. The strength of the eddies and whirlpools was such that it was in vain to oppose it with the force of the oars. *Mexicana* was carried on by the current to the northeast point of the Canal de Cardero with such violence that it appeared she would be cast away, but [the current being] blocked by the obstacle of the shore set away from it, and the two [goletas] followed the inlet with some effort. Because the tide had turned, they anchored in the anchorage of Viana in 34 fathoms gravel, at about a cable and a half from the shore.

It had been wet all day and although the aspect was promising the weather did not change. At night the squalls were repeated, and all appearances told that however persistent the northwesters had been, they had now settled in the southeast, thereby

---

[9] The last three paragraphs are omitted from the *Viage*. A different account is added to the next paragraph.

becoming favourable to our intention, bringing some benefit along with the great inconvenience of the rain in such incommodious ships.

Some Indian canoes were at the sides of the ships, and the relations were the same as we had with those we knew. Among their protections from the rain, the Indians brought leather helmets with painted stripes, of which they traded us one. We also saw a canoe larger than any we had seen thus far, which crossed from one shore to the other and did not turn to let us see it. [10]

[10] This and the preceding paragraph are omitted from the *Viage*.

XII

The goletas weigh, then anchor in the entrance of the Canal de Nuevos Remolinos, not knowing whether it was closed: The launch is made ready to lead the goletas: They follow the launch, and new entries presenting themselves, they make the anchorage of Novales: Valdés leaves in the launch and examines the Brazo del Canónigo and Brazo de Flores: The goletas weigh and proceed to the anchorage of Bauzá: For the first time natives who understand the language of Nutca are encountered: The anchorage of Cárdenas: Galiano leaves in the launch and explores the Arm named for him, and Valdés completes the examination of the Ensenada de Estrada: The goletas weigh and come to anchor in the anchorage of Insulto: Valdés leaves in the launch: Affront of the natives to our people ashore: Good conduct of our people: The delay of the launch starts to give concern, but it fortunately returns, having explored the mainland shores of the Brazos of Retamal, Vernacci, Balda, and Baldinat, and as far as the Canal de Pinedo.

At seven in the morning of the 27th [of July], we weighed, and with some wind from the east continued as far as the mouth of the Canal de Nuevos Remolinos.[1] In doubt whether it continued or whether it was closed we came to anchor on the north shore at its mouth, in a cove with a pretty meadow, where there were house frames of an abandoned village.[2] The launch was made ready with half a crew from each goleta, leading the way throughout. Passing the narrows in the middle section, we experienced more whirlpools, which subjected the goletas to the will of their force. We passed them with safety, and finding

---

[1] Literally, New [or More] Whirlpools.
[2] The *Viage* does not mention this village.

new entries to the north, took anchor in a good anchorage at eleven in the morning, which we called Novales. A latitude observation was made ashore, a time check was made, and the launch departed with Valdés to examine the entries which presented themselves to the north.

At ten in the morning of the 28th, Valdés returned, having examined the Brazo del Canónigo and Brazo de Flores, and [having determined] that the inlet continued westward. Immediately we weighed and made use of the tide until it turned against us and obliged us to anchor in twenty four fathoms mud in the anchorage of Bauzá.

The wind was calm during most of the day, and the scattered clouds started to drift away, promising a wind from the fourth quadrant. In the afternoon three canoes of Indians came, among whom some understood the Nutca language, especially one who acted as interpreter for trading. They knew Macuina and other Nutca chiefs, and from the way bargaining was conducted and the selection in trade of known equivalents, [they must have] traded many times with those natives, and had positive information on our handling [of trade] and on our wants. They had a musket, probably acquired in that way, and some salmon which they traded to us. They gave a somewhat confused account of Wizanamish[sic] and of the Nuchimases, and their woven cloaks were of the same stuff, workmanship, and size as those of Nutca. We acquired much dried smoked salmon, of which the crew ate as they wished, leaving a large part for the succeeding days.[3]

In the morning of the 29th, with a steady west wind and an ingoing tide, we could tack, gaining considerably towards the entry to open water which we believed from our observation and calculations to be already close. The land had already taken a different aspect; it was smooth and low and left a large expanse of sky visible to the northwest. The shoreline was a sandy beach

---

[3] Most of this paragraph is omitted from the *Viage*.

with a good water depth,[4] not presenting the gloomy and horrific aspect of the high and mountainous shores we had left behind. The wind strengthened during the afternoon and raised a sea, but soon dropped and left us almost becalmed. There was no lack of Indians in canoes all day, who by trade increased our supply of fresh and smoked salmon, in exchange for some trifles, iron, and shells. In general they had no news of Macuina or of the Nuchimases.[5]

All day we were tacking back and forth, and gained the anchorage of Cárdenas at four in the afternoon, where an entry presented itself to the north. We anchored in twelve fathoms fine gravel, in order to send the launch to explore the inlet, which according to information from the boat extended far to the northeast.

In the morning of the 30th, Galiano left in the launch for the exploration of the Canal de Cárdenas, and soon after Vernacci [left] in the boat to explore the Ensenada de Estrada, which we had left to the east, since although we had seen it to be closed from the goletas our doubts would not be satisfied until verification by a prolix examination from a closer distance had removed any illusion.[6]

The launch returned at five in the morning, having explored the Brazo de Cárdenas, and the boat soon after looking at the bay. We observed the latitude on the beach, with both the natural and artificial horizons, and soon, taking advantage of circumstances which on the previous day had been so favourable for us, we set sail on a fresh easterly wind, running along the north shore at a distance which would not let any hole capable of letting pass a canoe escape [our notice] . At sunset[7]

---

[4] Sondables. There is no precise equivalent in English. This one word means a place where there is enough water to sail but the bottom is within reach of the anchor cable, a combination met infrequently on the west coast.

[5] This paragraph shortened in the *Viage*.

[6] This paragraph seems to be inserted solely to point out to the authorities that Galiano was carrying out his instructions. The Ensenada can only be a small indentation in the shoreline, or possibly Blenkinsop Bay. The decision of the editor of the *Viage* to delete the paragraph can be understood.

an inlet was seen, and the goletas anchored in the anchorage of Insulto,[8] so that the launch could make new explorations.

As soon as we anchored, various canoes came to our sides. Most of the natives understood the Nutca language, and showed that they had traded a great deal with Europeans who had different trade goods with which they had exchanged. The Chief[9] had a hat much like another seen on the voyage of the previous year of the corvettes *Descubierta* and *Atrevida* which was held in particular esteem by the Ankau[10] of Mulgrave,[11] because he had won it from his enemies in battle.[12] The chief at Insultos traded it to us, and it was the only one we could acquire because being completely hesitant rather than cautious in their sales, they disdained whatever was offered to them other than those things which had a known use, which could appeal to their tastes and had a real value. Apparently their goods [to trade] were limited to some fish, harpoons with which they kill them, and a sea otter skin, which we were eager to acquire, in order that experts could compare its quality with those from farther north or south.[13]

None of them was permitted to come aboard; however, through some carelessness on the part of those who were keeping watch over their activities, they stole some trifles which they tucked away just before they went off. Their manner was freer and less constrained than that of the other savages we had seen, their look daring, and their ease [of manner] spoke of a proud character. They left us at nightfall, promising to return the next morning.[14]

---

[7] Four in the afternoon in the *Viage*.

[8] The name means an affront.

[9] The word "cacique" is used here, rather than "tais," which is used in the *Viage*.

[10] Sic. Ankau is a Tlingit word the Spanish understood to mean chief.

[11] A cove on the east shore of Yakutat Bay, Alaska. Malaspina's expedition spent some time there in 1791.

[12] Galiano was not on the 1791 voyage; all his officers as well as the artist Cardero had been. This suggests that someone other than Galiano wrote this sentence, although Galiano could have written what the others told him.

[13] This sentence omitted from the *Viage*.

[14] Paragraph omitted from the *Viage*.

At dawn on the 31st Vernacci left in the launch to explore the aforesaid arm to the north, in case it should lead to the sea, which we believed to be quite near. He carried chronometer 344 and the artificial horizon. Meanwhile our people went ashore to gather wood and to replace oars for the goleta, and we went with them to make observations, which we stopped soon because of a sudden rainfall, with no promise of any clearing.[15]

At midday they shouted from ashore that the Indians had attacked our people, and we saw all the canoes gathered in the place where the workers were. Immediately Salamanca embarked in the boat with armed men and went to their rescue, warned not to harm the natives, unless driven to extremities in their own defence, and then to inflict the least possible harm. A round was fired [from one of the ship's guns] with ball to intimidate them with the noise, and they immediately embarked in their canoes, crossing the inlet at some distance from the goletas towards the opposite shore.

Seeing that the boat would not overtake them quickly, and knowing they had not harmed our people, nor taken anything of consequence, we did not pursue them. The boat went ashore and picked up the people. As soon as they were aboard, a round was fired with ball at elevation, to make the Indians see that they were not as safe as they thought. It passed over them, and the Indians quickened their paddling, in haste to distance themselves from the goletas and gain the opposite shore.[16]

At the time of the affront there were six men ashore, one with a musket for use in hunting, and the Indians resolved to steal this weapon from him. One of the Indians wished to take the musket for hunting, but the sailor not wishing to let it go, the Indians wanted to take it by force. Our people made ready to defend themselves, and the Indians faced them, drawing their knives, but our people resorted to sabres and without using their

---

[15] It appears from the next paragraph that the officers then returned to the ship in the boat.

[16] Paragraph omitted from the *Viage*.

blades on them made their way to the beach with blows. [17] This gave them a clear indication that arms would be used only as far as necessary for self defence. The seamen having complied so well with their orders on this day, we had the satisfaction of having avoided, by their conduct, shedding the blood of those miserable people given over to their passion and greed. Our people's conduct could be envied by the greatest philosopher, making the most worthy pronouncements of humanity in cool blood from his office. [18]

It cleared up after midday, and we returned ashore to continue the observations. In a short time a canoe came in view from the west, with only two Indians, sticking close to the shore, and arriving very near us. They disembarked on the beach and took from the woods some belongings that they had abandoned in their hurry. They came alongside with some confidence and asked us by signs when we would leave, without their manner being any more submissive, although they saw in us some annoyance and displeasure. They went away soon, still repeating that we should go away at once. [19]

It rained all day and night and our greatest concern was for the safety of the launch, on which perhaps this scuffle with the natives might recoil. [20] Most of the natives, besides their arrows and clubs were armed with knives one third to half a vara long[21] with double edges and a sharp point. We could carry out our explorations only with our frail launch, because the boat was needed for communication between the goletas and with the shore, and for our own defence. [22] The small capacity

---

[17] A sabre could be used either to cut with the edge, or sideways as a club. The latter mode was termed "a palos," the words used in the MS.

[18] During the late eighteenth century, the "filosofos" of the Enlightenment were much given to extolling the "noble savage" without ever having seen one. Galiano's criticism was a common one among explorers. Lapérouse wrote in almost identical terms about the natives in the South Pacific. This paragraph is much shortened in the *Viage*, eliminating the criticism of the philosophers.

[19] Paragraph omitted from the *Viage*.

[20] The verb used is "recalar", but "recular" must be meant.   [21] 0.3 to 0.4 metres.

[22] There is no mention of the canoe purchased from the Indians and later described as unserviceable. Perhaps it had been abandoned.

of the launch limited its armament to some small firearms and sabres, not putting much trust in the former because the rain did not leave much confidence in their use. The natives started to be numerous and warlike, and one could expect that the passion for possessing our arms would place them in the position of sparing no action to attain them. These reflections increased our concern for Vernacci, and the people under his command.[23]

On the morning of the 1st [of August] two Indians came in a canoe, saying they were from a different village to those who had affronted us on the previous day. They carried a well cared for musket, a lance with an iron tip three quartos long[24] and some wide knives of the same metal, with a groove along the middle of the blade, and altogether similar to those used by the Indians of Mulgrave.[25] They freely gave them to us to examine and told us they had made them in the same way the Tujunes[26] had explained to us. It was not possible to trade anything with them; they asked only for powder. They gave us to understand they were Nuchimases. They were on shore with us while we observed them, and soon left without reappearing all day.

It rained heavily in the afternoon. The downpour was of extraordinary strength and hardly let up for a moment before returning in full fury. Our boat had to be baled continuously, and our launch was on all our minds. The wind was gusty but never hard, and the mist reduced the visibility to hardly a cable. During the night it rained continuously, although not as heavily as in the afternoon.[27]

The morning of the 2nd [of August] was clear, and allowed us to make latitude observations with both the natural and

---

[23] Paragraph much shortened in the *Viage*.

[24] The quarto or cuarto was the width across the extended fingers of a hand. Its value was never standardized, but might have been about 20 cm. The unit was already obsolete in 1792.

[25] Another indication that someone other than Galiano contributed to the narrative.

[26] The name of the tribe at Mulgrave, given as "Tejunues" in Novo y Colson. This sentence is omitted from the *Viage*.

[27] Paragraph omitted from the *Viage*.

artificial horizons. In the afternoon a squall came up rapidly, ending with a great downpour during all the afternoon and a great part of the night. No Indians appeared, which increased our concern.

The 3rd was exactly the same, except that in the afternoon there was lightning and thunder. The mercury of the artificial horizons had been affected by moisture, and to make use of it we tried to separate [the water.] Various ways [being] ineffective, we decided to boil it in a pot. This started to achieve the effect, when the man doing the job felt himself overcome by severe pain and fever, followed by a heavy sweat.[28] Some others were slightly ill from the same cause, and we then had to abandon our operation.[29] In the afternoon some Indians came, who took pains to explain that they were not those with whom we had had the disturbance. We gave them some oddments, and they showed us their gratitude, cutting strips from a sea otter skin they carried, and making us presents of this kind.[30]

On the 4th the weather appeared to be established in the same pattern as on previous days, since at the same times we were in the same circumstances. A canoe came alongside with Cauti, a chief[31] who was, according to what he told us, powerful in this region. He brought us word of the launch, and also of Macuina, Nazapé, and other Nutca chiefs.[32] Cauti's carriage and manner testifed to his high rank. It appeared to us that to gain the friendship and trust of this chief would lead to the security of our launch, and for this [reason] we gave him ample presents from both ships. He offered to return, and said that Sisiakis should also come, [a chief who was] his equal, ruler of the land along the shores to the north.

The next morning this chief[33] came. We treated him with the most thorough courtesy, as the situation of our launch required. He said he was going to sleep ashore and return the following day to receive the presents we offered him.

---

[28] The *Viage* adds that he was fifty years old.

[29] The *Viage* says the sick man recovered after a while.

[30] Last two sentences omitted from the *Viage*.

[31] Cacique.   [32] Gefes.   [33] Sisiakis.

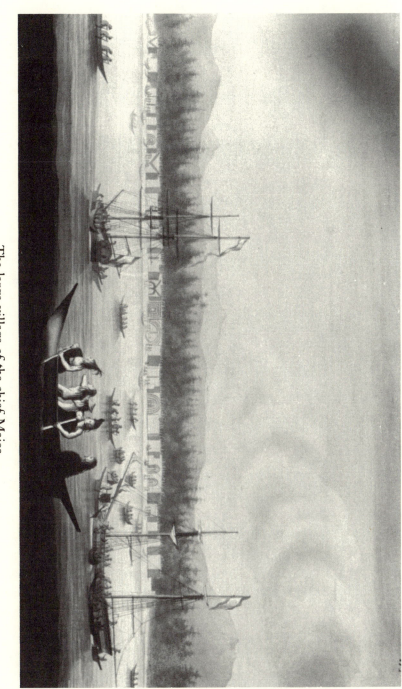

The large village of the chief Majoa
on the east coast of Vancouver Island.
Sutil is at the left, and *Mexicana* at the right.

Courtesy of Museo de América, Madrid.

We were by then much concerned for the safety of the launch, considering it to be short of provisions, which we judged would be damaged in the struggle against persistent hard weather and continuous rain, and [considering it] to be among a numerous and daring Indian population. Thus, we extended ourselves in our cordiality and gifts to Sisiakis, whose help could be very useful in some unhappy circumstance. This Indian spoke the language of Nutca very clearly, and his confidence, ease, and lack of mistrust reflected his nobility and power, which he exaggerated. He ascribed an inferior rank to Cauti, and said he knew no equal in these lands, all of which he said belonged to him. He offered to regale us when we should visit his village, according to the custom of the taises, who did not trade, except under the guise of making presents, but in the end he abandoned this policy, injecting himself into the negotiations for some pelts brought by his people. To those who had rewarded him profusely, he also showed his interest and greed, even though he apologized for these traits in his Indians, and said only he should make presents in his house. He showed clear ideas of having seen large ships with three masts, although he did not tell us when, or in what place.[34]

He left by the large entry leading to the WNW, and one of the canoes of his people crossed to the south shore, from which we inferred that they were [some] of the Indians who lived there and who had attacked us, although Sisiakis, fearing our just animosity towards them, painted our attackers as despicable and ill intentioned.[35]

The Indians had some muskets, a bag of ammunition, and a powder horn. Although the rain was less copious than in the preceding days there was no time of day nor any interval when it did not occur.

---

[34] The trading activities are omitted from the *Viage*.

[35] This passage taken from AGN Hist. 558. MN MS 619 says that the canoes "crossed to the south shore, from which we knew many of the Indians had come, although Sisiakis, fearing our just animosity towards them, painted our attackers as despicable and ill intentioned." The AGN version seems more reasonable.

On the 6th the wind continued to be extremely variable, and there were continual showers during the afternoon and night.

By then the launch was giving us the utmost concern. The time had gone by for which they had taken provisions, and at best they must have been suffering a shortage. Since they had not come [back] aboard to alleviate this, we should fear some mishap. We started to consider ways of searching for them, and there seemed to be no better course than to leave *Mexicana* at the anchorage, in case the launch should return by another channel, while *Sutil* followed the mainland firing guns, and seeking word from the Indians. However, the appearance of the launch at seven in the morning of the 7th through the entry to the west relieved our embarrassment and caused us heartfelt joy.[36] We learned that they had not laid down the oars for a day and a half, during which time they had nothing to eat, drink, or smoke. They had decided that if they were further delayed in finding us they would go to a village and provision themselves, trying to effect a trade, but if politeness failed using force, even though they would be obliged to make a satisfactory restitution later.[37]

The weather had tenaciously obstructed all their plans, and the continuous fog and downpours were obstacles to linking up the mainland shore. Still, they followed it through the Canales de Retamal, Vernacci, Balda, and Baldinat, and completed their exploration in the Canal de Pinedo, which is to the west of the last. They did this six days after leaving the goletas, already almost out of provisions, and having suffered the inconveniences of a lack of shelter available in the launch or along the shores they had explored.[38]

The Indian population in this area was large, particularly in

---

[36] The *Viage* says they did not see the launch until it was close by, because of fog.

[37] The *Viage* omits the last sentence.

[38] The *Viage* adds a latitude observation here, followed by four paragraphs describing the launch voyage in detail, mentioning Vernacci a number of times. Boat parties sent out by Galiano made sketch maps of the route as they proceeded. A few of these are still to be found, in MN MS2456. Some of them have an account of the journey and the terrain written right on the sketches, which have been incorporated in the narrative of the voyage. It is possible that the account in the *Viage* was taken from notes on Vernacci's sketches, which are not in MS 2456.

the Brazo de Vernacci and Brazo de Balda, in which there was a populous village whose inhabitants were bright and proud, since the remaining baubles and trade goods carried in the launch were there exhausted without the equivalent being obtained. The Indians showed their displeasure, not taking a good view of the exploration of the closed inlets where they and their families lived, which [exploration] they could not attribute to the simple curiosity which was their usual motive.[39]

The launch did not return by the route by which it had left, from which they had departed to find a shorter one and to increase geographic knowledge. They returned by way of an archipelago of islands which gave great confusion in the direction to be taken, for which reason they followed the Canal de Torres, rounded its southwest point and rejoined the goletas.

At the outlet of the Canal de Torres, the launch had seen a gulf, ending to the west in a multitude of islands, which they soon conjectured contained channels leading to the sea.[40] By then the resemblance [of the terrain] we had found to the part that had been explored did not indicate any useful or prudent exploration, to [which we should] expose a frail launch, among a numerous Indian population, risking the loss of the security enjoyed until then. In addition, we should not place goletas of such light burthen, and so defective in their construction, in the position of staying in such high latitudes with the equinox approaching. It appeared more interesting to use the time remaining in our campaign in exploring the Entrada de Ezeta, and fixing the location of some points on the coast from Fuca to the south, particularly those in the Channel of Santa Bárbara.[41] The above-mentioned corvettes[42] had not examined the islands during the expedition of the previous year, but had seen some of those which formed the channel, whose location disagreed with that shown on our old maps. Leaving uncorrected [the location

---

[39] This is a much abbreviated account of the launch voyage, in comparison with the *Viage*.

[40] The gulf was Queen Charlotte Strait.

[41] The last was the only one of these objectives which was attained.

[42] *Descubierta* and *Atrevida*.

A view of the Canal de Bernaci, or Vernacci, now Knight Inlet. Juan Vernacci explored it during a seven-day boat expedition.

Courtesy of Museo de América, Madrid.

of] the islands not seen, the courses through the channel would vary [from those indicated by the map]. There was no way to form a map of this part of our Americas except to finally locate all the said islands.[43]

All these considerations made us choose the plan of seeking in the first place the exit to the sea, and to prefer our projected operations to the exploration of the arms and channels so plentiful on the coast. However, although the day presented opportunities the goletas could follow, we had to sacrifice them to give the boat crew of *Mexicana's* launch some rest, which they much needed.

---

[43] In simpler terms, Galiano had decided to break off his explorations of the coast. He has made use of Malaspina's instructions, which cautioned him about safety and mentioned the examination of the points south of Nootka as cited by Galiano.

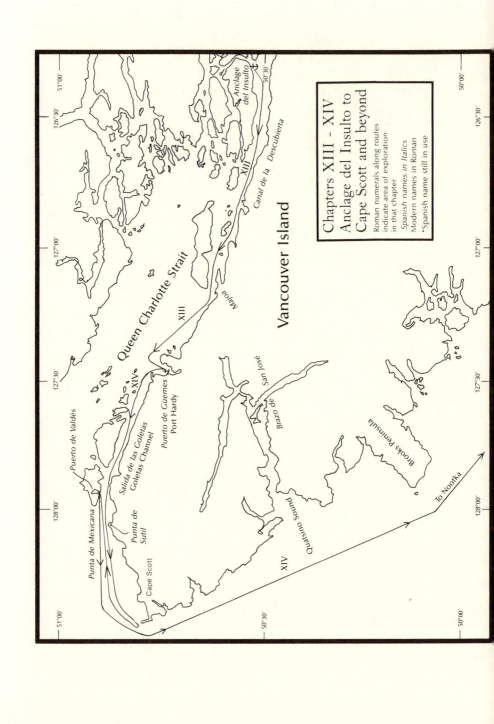

Chapters XIII - XIV
Anclage del Insulto to
Cape Scott and beyond

Roman numerals along routes
indicate area of exploration
in that chapter

Spanish names in Italics
Modern names in Roman
*Spanish name still in use

Vancouver Island

Queen Charlotte Strait

Canal de la Descubierta

Anclage
del Insulto

XIII

Mateoa

XIII

Puerto de Valdés

Salida de las Goletas
Goletas Channel

XIV

Puerto de Güemes
Port Hardy

San José

Brazo de

Punta de Mexicana

Punta de
Sutil

Cape Scott

XIV

Quatsino Sound

Brooks Peninsula

To Nootka

51°00'
126°30'
127°00'
127°30'
128°00'
51°00'

50°30'
50°00'
126°30'
127°00'
127°30'
128°00'
50°00'
50°30'

XIII

The goletas weigh and follow the Canal de Descubierta in which they anchor: They weigh again and pass by the village of Sisiakis: The wealth of the Indians in sea otter skins becomes apparent: The English brig Venus *is sighted: Information on this ship: The goletas anchor between the village of Majoa, and that of Quacos in the Canal de la Atrevida: They weigh again and aim to explore the coast to the north, but the overcast prevents this and they come to anchor in the anchorage of Rozadero: The cables are damaged and they go on to the harbour of Güemes.*

On the 8th [of August], at six in the morning, we raised our anchors and took to the oars, [at first] making use of the tide, and soon afterwards the sails, beating to windward. The wind was extremely variable in its strength, direction, and quality, and although the sun was out, a penetrating cold was felt, which obliged us to put on heavier clothing. At three in the afternoon there was a violent gust in which we furled our topgallant sails, and soon after *Mexicana* [furled] its topsails.[1] Very soon it fell calm, and stayed so for the rest of the afternoon and night.[2]

We intended to anchor at nightfall by the islands on the north shore where the boat found 32 fathoms gravel, but the bottom was so irregular and steep that *Mexicana* had 15 fathoms at the stern and 30 at the bow. It was the same for us; we let go the anchor on [a sounding of] 40 and it did not hit bottom at 55, so we had to row with the anchor hanging until it caught. We led a

---

[1] *Mexicana* had no topgallant sails.

[2] This paragraph shortened in the *Viage*.

cable ashore to guard against whatever current or land breeze might catch us with the anchor off the bottom. On the 9th at five thirty in the morning, we set sail on a steady fresh east wind. With this at our stern we overcame the tide, which all morning was against us. We sailed among an archipelago of islands, following the channels [lying] more to the WNW.

Sisiakis came alongside with two of his Indians, giving us to understand that Nutca lay to the southeast, and that we could arrive there quickly by sea. He asked us to come by his village, where we could sleep, saying that he would give us a feast and his women would serve us, as they had other voyagers. No doubt, by the unequivocal gestures he made, the English merchants and shipowners had paid them with a great quantity of copper for this fine welcome.

We soon saw his large village, on a hill in an amphitheatre, surrounded by a pleasant meadow.[3] Here he redoubled his offers and importunities that we should stop, and as soon as it was realized that we were determined not to lose time on our way, they went to their village. Immediately fifty Indians came off in a number of canoes, with various sea otter skins to trade and some cloaks woven from tree bark[4] and grass, worked in colours forming a very symmetrical and tasteful border. We took one for the King.

From ten in the morning we had seen a brig to the west. We arrived within hailing distance in the afternoon and learned it was the *Venus*, Captain Henrique Sheperd, come from Bengal, having touched at Fuca and at Nutca, in which establishments they had spoken with our ships. They gave us the sad news that at the former place the Indians had killed the second in command of the frigate *Princesa*, who was Pilot of the Navy Don Antonio Serantes, and that the commandant, Fidalgo, had been obliged in justice to kill many Indians,[5] that the frigate *Ger-*

---

[3] *The Viage* adds a description of the painted house fronts and the village.

[4] This would have been the inner bark of the red cedar.

[5] Fidalgo's superiors did not agree; he was severely reprimanded. See: Kendrick, 1985. The comment on Fidalgo is omitted from the *Viage*.

trudis had gone from Nutca to Fuca, and that when *Venus* left [Nutca] eight days earlier, there remained only the Spanish brig *Activa*, and the English storeship *Dedalo*, which brought supplies for Captain Vancouver.[6] The brig carried only 22 men, mostly negroes and mulattos, badly clothed and very clumsy at shiphandling, in spite of there being nothing [that could be] cleaner and lighter than the brig, which had a graceful hull. A net two yards high surrounded the ship, to prevent any surprise from the Indians, and on board were various swivel guns and four small cannons.

Night had started to fall by then, so we anchored the three ships between the large village of Quacos and that of Majoa.[7] The facades of their dwellings, which appeared to be quite spacious, were covered with paintings and carvings. From one or another of these dwellings many canoes hurried to our side, and in one was the tais Majoa, who announced himself by presenting a [sea otter] skin to each of the commanders of the ships, bringing a quantity of various other good ones. We traded for some of them, more in response to their urging then for any gain provided by goods which were cheaper in the Presidios of California, free of the risk of damage between the two places. A sheet of copper weighing fourteen pounds was the price for which we could get one good skin and another of medium quality. Thus, the English shipowner, however cheap and economical his expeditions, was left with little profit from this trade, even though direct trade with Canton or Bengal provides all possible advantages.[8]

On board, we were being careful to avoid any altercation with the Indians, when a casual accident made us realize our exposure through the lack of understanding in the resolute and hot tempered character of the seaman, and through the intolerance

---

[6] The ship movements are omitted from the *Viage*.

[7] Galiano's map lacks accuracy in this region. The two villages are shown close together, and it is likely that Majoa was south of the west end of Malcolm Island, perhaps at the site of a modern Indian Reserve. Quacos is farther west.

[8] The last clause is omitted from the *Viage*.

and violence of the Indians.[9] One of our people had a dispute with an Indian, who immediately asked one of the others in the canoes for a knife and came right on board the goleta to confront the seaman. He found the seaman expecting him with a sabre already drawn. All the Indians became upset and began to ask for their tais, who was in the cabin. It cost a good deal [of effort] to quiet them, both at the time and right until their departure at nightfall. We needed to use the greatest care to show them goodwill, but without trusting them; taking care that they should not crowd aboard the ships, yet without holding them back in a suspicious way.[10] These Indians are good looking and well made, their mien proud, and their carriage easy. They did not bring any of their women, however much they had promised their availability if we went to their villages, citing the custom of other voyagers.

At dawn on the 10th, we set sail towards the north shore to explore and locate it. On getting through the Canal de la Atrevida, [we found that] it ended at the west in many islands, which appeared to be the exit to the sea. The weather was cloudy with rain, and although the fresh southeast wind offered us the chance to make some running fixes[11] to make a chart, the low visibility over the land prevented this. In effect we arrived at noon a half mile from the north shore, and found many islets. The southeast wind beat upon them, continuing to strengthen, with cloud and rain, for which reason we turned towards the south shore to take anchor in its shelter. The wind was slackening as we approached it, so we steered for a beach to seek an anchorage, and started to pick up the bottom in 25 fathoms fine brown sand. We approached to a cable and a half from the shore, anchoring in 7 fathoms sand, and leading a line ashore to

---

[9] The *Viage* attributes the incident only to the violence of the Indians.

[10] Sentence omitted in the *Viage*.

[11] A running fix was made by taking successive bearings on an object and recording the direction and distance the ship had travelled between them. To be accurate, this requires a good estimate of the course made good and the distance run, which was hardly possible with only a compass and a log line to go by.

take better shelter, leaving the ship's hull in 6 fathoms, sand and barnacles.

During the night there was a lot of rain, the wind rose, and the surge was so strong that the goletas pitched [enough] to take in water forward. The wind slackened at dawn and we recovered the cables, finding them damaged. We weighed immediately to improve our anchorage. The wind was light from the southeast, the rain never stopped, and the shore was covered with low cloud. We followed it after clearing the islets which we kept to the northwest, and finding a bay a short way off we entered it under oars, the wind being almost calm. The boat went around it in search of an anchorage and found one on the east side in 22 fathoms muddy sand. We came to anchor, and later moved to a cove farther to the east. We named this harbour Güemes, as a courtesy to His Excellency Don Juan Vicente de Güemes, Count of Revillagigedo, patron of our commission.

This harbour has another cove in its southwest part, but it would serve only for vessels of light draft, because of a shoal at its entrance. The best anchorage for heavier ships is in the southeast part. The north shore is foul ground, but has a river of good water on it, and there is no lack of convenient places to take on water in various places along the shore. The goletas did this in a bay close to the south of where we lay.[12] The shore offers a good beach, where one can take exercise, and is fruitful in anti-scorbutics, among them the Quilite,[13] a very tasty species of spinach.

---

[12] Sentence omitted from the *Viage*.

[13] "Quelite" is a name given in Mexico to various edible green plants which grow in the wild.

XIV

Stay in the Puerto de Güemes: The launch leaves to explore the Canal de la Salida de las Goletas: The goletas weigh, and the weather looking bad take anchor at Meir, later at Villavicencio: They emerge into the sea and anchor in the gulf between Punta de Sutil and Cabo Scot: Because of a storm they return to Puerto de Valdés, and make their voyage to Nutca when it has passed.

It rained continuously all day and night [on August 11th], with the wind in the second quadrant,[1] and continued thus on the 12th, with a number of gusts from the east. In spite of this our situation was secure, and the sea responded abundantly to the fishermen with sole, salmon, halibut,[2] and a great abundance of small fish similar to the cod of Malvinas and Puerto Deseado.

Our stay in this harbour was a long one. The wind, settled in the southeast with continual downpours, did not permit us to move our location. We considered ourselves to be very close to the exit to the sea, and it was inappropriate to choose such bad weather for the departure,[3] all the more when we could use the time to correct our chronometers precisely, making use of the clear intervals offered by the sky. The goletas had frayed one of their principal mooring lines in the last anchorage, and there remained only one [which was] satisfactory plus the hemp hawser, which made up the three which had been allowed for

---

[1] Between east and south.　　　　　[2] Rayas, probably halibut.
[3] The *Viage* says they wanted good weather to examine the outer coast south of Cape Scott.

the ships. For this [reason] also we could not expose ourselves in search of an anchorage close to the exit in unsafe weather.

We also used the time of our stay to make geodetic studies, and to take exercise on the western beach of the harbour when weather permitted, making use of an opportunity conducive to good health, which the steep shores of the channels inside had denied us.[4]

Our dealings with the Indians during this time afforded us some salmon. Their fishery was in the bay to the southwest, where there were some houses which appeared to be abandoned. They came to the goletas to make their trades, leaving as soon as these were completed. There were no more than eight who visited us in four canoes. They looked more stupid than those of the villages of Sisiakis, Majoa, and Insulto; however we understood they were Nuchimases, and belonged to [the village of] Majoa.[5]

The regulation of the chronometers being dealt with, Galiano left on the 22nd in the launch to follow the channel leading to the west, with the object of finding a good anchorage close to the exit to the sea so that the situation of the goletas could be improved and they could make use of the first occasion when the wind was northwest to proceed to Nutca. He ran along the length of the south shore of the Canal de Salida[6] without finding an anchorage, as far as the Puerto de Gorostiza, beyond which he observed latitude and east west hour angles from Punta de Sutil, and very close to it he made use of an artificial horizon made of the crew's wine, since the mercury had been forgotten.[7] In this way he determined the location of the mouth of the Canal de la Salida de las Goletas.

In the morning we were favoured with fresh east and southeast winds, although with the discomfort of the rains which

---

[4] Paragraph omitted from the *Viage*.

[5] The *Viage* ascribes the "stupidity" of these people to their small numbers and to their isolation.

[6] "Salida" means an exit. The choice of this name may be an echo of Article 2 of Revillagigedo's instructions.

[7] The use of the wine is omitted from the *Viage*.

usually accompany them. In the afternoon there were calms and some light airs from the west. The sky cleared, and with these advantages, the launch arrived at the goletas at eleven thirty at night.

On this excursion an Indian village was seen by the Punta de Sutil, from which two canoes came to the place of the observatory. The Indians treated them with the greatest friendliness, and admiringly exercised their curiosity at the sight of the instruments which they saw in use. In the Puerto de Güemes the wind had remained calm all day, and the fishing was just as successful as on previous days. [8]

On the 23rd we raised anchors looking to reach the harbour of Gorostiza, going along first under oars, then under sail as soon as the light wind settled in the east, which gradually shifted to become a headwind during the morning until noon, when it fell calm. Soon afterwards we had a west wind, with hard gusts, squalls, and low visibility. Around four in the afternoon, the sky and horizon took on the worst appearance and the wind and mist increased. Not being able to make the anchorage which was still three leagues away, we were forced into a decision to put back to the harbour we had left, so as not to pass the night tacking in a narrow channel in a storm which seemed to be building up. After we had fallen off, the wind dropped, and the mist cleared. The sky took on a better appearance, so we decided not to lose the advantage we had acquired, looking for another anchorage along the shore to await the dawn. With the help of the boat we found one in 27 fathoms gravel, let fall the anchor, and led another line ashore. The night was calm and serene. This place is marked on the map with the name of Meir.

At daylight we got under way under oars, until at nine the wind settled in the west. We made some progress by beating to windward all morning, which we started to lose from midday. However, determined not to lose what we had gained, on one

---

[8] Paragraph omitted from the *Viage*.

tack we sent off the boat to the north shore, in order to examine and sound a mooring place which offered itself there. It proved to be very commodious and secure, and we proposed to make for it as soon as *Mexicana* could join us. We hove to and fell off somewhat, [losing ground] which we recovered with difficulty, tacking between mid channel and the north shore until, being half a mile to leeward of the anchorage, we furled all sail and arrived [at the anchorage] with the oars, dropping anchor in 25 fathoms sand and gravel, in a bay which was named Villavicencio. Night fell with a very bright sky and clear horizons, but in a short time it clouded over and some showers fell, after which the whole night was peaceful.

In the morning we left under oars to make for the exit, and the fresh wind soon settled in the east. We were making good time when at about nine we saw a sloop along the north shore in the anchorage we named Balandra[9] which we did not recognize because they did not reply with their flag to ours. The sun was obscured and did not permit an observation, but the entry had already been fixed satisfactorily. To locate it exactly *Sutil* followed the north shore very closely, while *Mexicana* followed the south one. *Sutil's* boat explored the Cala de Consolación, and [also] an entry which offered a good harbour, close to the north point of Salida. This harbour was found in effect, with various sheltered and secure anchorages, and with a depth of 6 to 24 fathoms ooze and mud. Its east face was a tongue of land with an isthmus a cable wide, and with a sand and gravel beach as far as the open sea.[10] This harbour was called Valdés, in homage to His Excellency Don Antonio Valdés, Secretary of State and of the Navy Department, under whose ministry the navy had made such notable progress.[11]

Sutil waited for its boat while Salamanca was making his exploration of the harbour. On his return *Sutil* continued on to

---

[9] Meaning sloop. The anchorage is between Nigei and Hope Islands.

[10] Sentence omitted from the *Viage*.

[11] Antonio Valdés was Navy Minister for many years. He was an uncle of Cayetano Valdés.

An Indian from the north end of Vancouver Island
The Salida de las Goletas was the channel
followed by the goletas to the open sea.
It is still called Goletas Channel.
Courtesy of Museo de América, Madrid.

Punta Mexicana. Being close to it, various strands of kelp could be seen which came from the surf on the reef which jutted out into the sea, where it originated. We sounded in 6 fathoms rocky bottom, and crossed the channel towards Punta Sutil, sounding the entry to the channel of Salida, which was 14 fathoms deep in the middle, shallowing towards both shores. The strength and direction of the wind varied; the horizon and the sky were obscured. We hoped to see it in order to follow whatever plan appeared most suitable, but the wind, settling in the east and northeast, carried us out to sea.

As we were leaving the points, some six canoes turned up, with thirty four Indians, stronger and more formidable than all those we had seen before, and of a pleasing appearance. They were from the villages of the Punta de Sutil, and they invited us there with signs, but did not come to our side, however much we welcomed them.[12]

After nightfall, the wind blowing fresh from the ESE, we followed the inshore tack, seeing the land by the light of the moon. We sounded each half hour, and found a constant depth of 30 fathoms fine black sand. The land gave shelter from the wind, and our situation was most opportune to continue our tasks in the morning. For these reasons we anchored at eleven fifteen at night, veering 30 fathoms of cable. Knowing we were dragging [the anchor] we gradually veered more, changing the place where the cable was being chafed,[13] until we were riding on 110 fathoms. The chop from the southwest made us roll heavily, with the bow pointed ESE into the wind, from which direction it did not stop blowing all night. We took the waves broadside, at times over the gunwale.[14]

At daylight the sky was cloudy and threatening. We raised the anchor and followed the inward tack, sounding until we were a

---

[12] This and the previous paragraph are omitted from the *Viage*.

[13] This long phrase is covered by the word "refrescando." In nautical English, this is called "freshening the nip."

[14] The last three sentences are omitted from the *Viage*.

little more than half a mile off, in 16 fathoms gravel. We ran along the shore as far as Cabo Scot, the wind continuing to strengthen from the southeast.

As soon as we left the narrows between Cabo Scot and the Islas de Lanz we realized how heavy the wind was at sea, and when we came upon this the wind shifted more to the south, [at a time] when Cabo Scot lay in this direction. Already reduced to no more than the two courses,[15] we preferred in these circumstances to pass the time in the shelter of the land. We turned away from the wind, and under courses with the wind in the SSE we steered close to the shore, and as soon as we left Cabo Scot bearing S 1/4 SW we hove to under main and fore staysail.

The wind strengthened to the extent that we had to keep the mainsail double reefed, and at times such strong gusts came that we could not carry even this sail. We intended to pass this time in the shelter of the land to make use of the favourable northwest winds which usually follow, but far from clearing up, the sky took on a more unpleasant appearance. Considering that if, as it appeared, the wind continued in the south we would be set far to the north, lose the shelter of the land, and move away from our destination, we decided to return to the channel and make the Puerto de Valdés.[16]

To be able to attain this objective, we put this plan into effect at two in the afternoon, using all the sail the goletas could carry. As soon as we got inside, the wind and sea gradually subsided. We arrived at the entry at five in the afternoon with a following tide of some strength, with whirlpools. We were quickly able to make the harbour in three tacks, with an east wind, since as soon as we reached the channel we found the wind coming from this direction.[17]

The night was rough; the wind blew with much force, and

---

[15] The lowest sail on each mast.

[16] Most of the last two paragraphs is omitted from the *Viage*.

[17] The *Viage* embellishes this passage with a description of the solitary and sombre aspect of the coast, and adds a paragraph on the approaches to the harbour.

the surf we could hear on the sea shore indicated the storm which prevailed outside, and from which we had escaped.

On the 27th the wind dropped, but the rain and cloud continued. Two Indian canoes came, loaded with sole of an enormous size, one of the largest was weighed and found to amount to 22 1/2 libras.[18] We did not notice any difference between these Indians and others in their dealings. They went away as soon as they had finished trading, leaving by the channel.[19]

We went in the launch to the extremity of the bay, and crossed the tongue of land, reaching the beach of the open ocean by a well beaten path through the heavy forest. On the beach we found tracks of bear and deer, but saw none of these animals. The low visibility did not permit us to make out some islands which had been seen from the goletas at a distance in the NNW.

The 28th was also obscured until nightfall, when the wind, which had settled in the northwest, cleared the atmosphere. On the 29th at eight thirty in the morning, we set sail on the first of the ebb, and tacked until we were carried out of the channel.[20]

The wind was weak from the west throughout the day and night, for which reason we did not make Cabo Scot until eight in the morning, following which we passed the narrows between the Islas de Lanz and the coast on a fresh NNW wind, making running fixes to locate points which came in view. At noon we were abreast of a bay which according to the English Captain Hanna[21] divided into two arms and is called San José.[22] In the afternoon the wind strengthened greatly, and we were afraid of losing the boat and launch, which were being towed astern,

---

[18] A libra is about equal to an English pound weight. If these fish were sole or flounder, they were indeed enormous. It is likely they were small halibut.

[19] This probably means that they went east along Goletas Channel, rather than towards the open sea.

[20] The *Viage* gives the date as the 30th of August.

[21] An English fur trader who was on the coast in 1785 and 1786.

[22] This was Quatsino Sound. The bay now called San Josef is a smaller bay just south of Cape Scott.

and which we saved by bringing them aboard at the cost of some risk. We were near Cabo Boisé or Frondoso at nightfall and saw another entry, which could only be Puerto Brooks, which was placed in such an erroneous position by the English Captain Colnet.[23] At this point we were on the shores located by the corvettes *Descubierta* and *Atrevida*, so during the night we made use of the wind, which continued very strong, under full sail. We reached a point off Nutca by morning and anchored in this harbour at midday [on August 31st], gaining the harbour under oars with the aid of the tide.[24]

[23] A fur trader, whose ships and person were seized in 1789 by Martinez, precipitating the "Nootka affair."

[24] The *Viage*, having started this passage a day later than the manuscript, omits one night and arrives at the same date for anchoring at Nootka.

XV

Vessels which were at Nutca: Some reflections on the exploration of the inlets:
Plants and rocks collected there: An idea of the accuracy of the maps.

In this harbour we found Ship Captain Don Juan de la
Quadra [sic], who had remained with the brig *Activa* to carry
out the articles of the final convention made with England in
1789, having despatched the corvette *Aránzazu* on the————[1]
of June to carry out explorations to the north, the *Concepción* to
San Blas, and the frigate *Gertrudis* to Núñez Gaona, which
afterwards was to explore the coast as far as the harbour of San
Francisco.[2]

Discovery and *Chatham* had also arrived, having examined
the coast as far as 52° 30′ north latitude. The part extending from the Boca de Pinedo as far as Cabo Norte is copied
from their discoveries, which they had communicated to us
with the established freedom, in the same way as we did, giving
them copies of the parts they chose, to add to their maps. From
Cabo Norte to the termination of their explorations, they had
not found the coast as full of entries and arms as in the inside, since
they only found one inlet of some length. Their ships had
grounded southwest of Cabo Norte, running great risk of being
lost. *Discovery* had got off without damage, but *Chatham* had

---

[1] Blank in the MS.
[2] Expanded and varied in the *Viage*.

[now] unloaded to repair the damage it had sustained.[3] We congratulated each other with the most cordial expressions of friendship, thanking the English commanders and officers for the thought and concern they had maintained for our safety, the first question they had asked on their arrival at Nutca being for word of the goletas.

There was also the English storeship *Dedalo*, which had come from England to bring supplies for Mr. Vancouver. In the Sandwich Islands, this ship had had the misfortune of losing its captain and an astronomer who was to join Mr. Vancouver's expedition.[4] They had been assassinated by those ferocious Indians who had deprived the immortal Captain Cook of [his return to] Europe. The number of ships in the harbour was augmented by the English brig named *Hope*, which was about to set sail to continue trading for furs.

We arrived at Nutca four months less four days after our departure from it, occupying all that time in explorations which could serve only to satisfy curiosity and draw philosophical conclusions, but in no way of use to navigators. Only the part from the Salida de las Goletas as far as the village of Sisiakis could be used for navigation and for commerce, because harbours are available where furs can be delivered or provided. Beyond that village, very few harbours are to be found. No trade is offered, be it for the commerce that can be pursued close to the sea or be it for the principal branch of commerce, the sea otter, which does not penetrate the narrows of the channels, as can be deduced from not having seen these animals in them, and seeing them as soon as we approached the exit to the sea.[5]

The profit taken by the navigator Dixon from the fur trade on this coast excited the cupidity of navigators, considering the great profits resulting from it, which he published in the

---

[3] *Discovery* and *Chatham* grounded in separate encounters with reefs. Both ships were endangered, but got clear on the next tide. *Chatham's* keel and bottom were repaired at Nootka. See: Lamb, 1984.

[4] Richard Hergest and William Gooch. A seaman was also killed.

[5] Only the first sentence of this paragraph is included in the *Viage*.

narrative of his voyage. For various reasons the commerce of the fur trade had been subjected to different terms [to those experienced by Dixon.] The competition of English, Americans, and even the French, who invoked the profit motive, and of our ships which had the objective of exploration had greatly increased the price of pelts, while the greed of the Chinese government, always watchful not to tolerate a commercial deficit, first prohibited the import of furs in trade, then went on to forbid their use in those Dominions. This was the word received by the traders who had touched at Nutca. All confirmed the first part of the prohibition, in spite of which it had not been an obstacle, because it had been possible during this year to count 22 ships engaged in this traffic; 11 English, 8 Americans, 2 Portuguese and one French. The second [part of the prohibition] could have been invented for the ends of a particular merchant, to extract his own profit, buying pelts from the others at an attractive price.[6]

The small profit which the Indians had realized from our trade in copper had also contributed to lowering its price; already in Nutca one had to give a sheet of one half arroba [in weight][7] for a medium size prime quality pelt. The brief commerce conducted with [the Nutca] natives was at second hand, since the pelts which could be collected in nearby waters had been exhausted by competition. The Nutcas went through the forest to buy them from the Nuchimases, for resale to the Europeans, but even in the short trade we had with the Nuchimases in the Salida de las Goletas we could not succeed in getting them to give us three skins of ordinary quality for two sheets of copper weighing an arroba.[8]

Our concern that we could suffer some damage and would need to use some of the [copper] sheets we might have traded for the gratification of the Indians, always made us deny ourselves the opportunities we had to proceed to trade for skins. Nor did

---

[6] In the *Viage*, this paragraph is abbreviated and altered.

[7] About 5.5 kilograms.　　　　[8] 11 kg. This paragraph omitted from the *Viage*.

we want to exchange other articles which could be needed. The thickness of our [copper] sheets, which was one linea[9] gave them an advantage over the thin ones usually brought by the traders. In competition with the English brig *Venus*, off the village of Majoa, not one canoe went to that ship, despising its sheets, which although larger, only had the usual thickness for sheathing ships. This navigator, even not knowing the latest suggested provision of the Chinese government, gave a clear account of the small profit which he could retain from this trade.[10]

Navigators are brought to these shores only by the expectation of an assured profit. It is to be hoped that under present conditions they will leave, all the more when the occupation of commerce from Europe and Asia ought to lead them elsewhere, wherever an opening remains for them. [Such an opening exists because of] the absence of rivalry from France, precipitated to its ruin by its horrible dissensions, and whose political reestablishment cannot possibly be in the near future.[11]

The dress and customs of the Americanos [sic] who inhabit these interior inlets are not in the least different to those of Nutca. In this narrative we have touched on the difference of their characters, which for the most part inclined to kindliness. Only once they had attacked us, in spite of finding themselves so many times superior [in force] in their meetings with the launch, while on many occasions we had received from them services of the greatest humanity.[12]

The terrain of the coast can be divided into three parts; from the entry [of the Strait of Juan de Fuca] to the Canal de Rosario,[13] from there to Cárdenas, and thence to the Salida de las Goletas. Of these three, the centre part is the least populated and of the worst aspect, not appearing easy to cultivate, nor

---

[9] 2 mm. A linea is one twelfth of a pulgada.

[10] Most of this paragraph is omitted from the *Viage*.

[11] This paragraph does not appear in the *Viage*. In its place there is a different account of the fur trade.

[12] This and the next four paragraphs are omitted from the *Viage*.

[13] Georgia Strait. Presumably the northern end is meant.

offering any goods for trade. The others are better, but not sufficiently so to invite a settlement.

The climate is temperate, the thermometer standing between 15 and 22 degrees,[14] being from 15 to 17 at daybreak, rising to 20 or 22 from ten in the morning to two in the afternoon and dropping at sunset. Only in the early hours of the 27th of July did it fall to 13 degrees.

We have said that in the Canal de la Separación the mountains were formed from rocks without order on shifting ground, as if produced by an explosion. If volcanic rocks were to be found in abundance, it would give a physical demonstration that the eruption of volcanoes had formed such a strange configuration of shorelines and inlets, but only quite rarely are mountains resembling volcanoes found on this coast.[15] We had seen only the one in the mountains of Carmelo which are visible from the Seno de Gaston.

Although in the other two outer parts of the coast[16] the shore is low, particularly to the northwest, high mountains can be seen close by, which show the ruggedness of the land.

The plants and rocks we had collected are the following, as classified by the naturalist of the expedition of the commandant Quadra.[17]

Without an understanding of the language, studies of Indian customs could not be advanced, particularly studies of men who differ so much [from us] in their ideas. The small population of the inlets inside the Strait made our contacts infrequent. As it happened, in the anchorage of Separación, where we made more of a stopover, there was no population or trade; for this

[14] If the temperatures in this paragraph are on the Reaumur scale used in an earlier chapter, they seem high, being equivalent to 19 to 27 degrees Celsius.

[15] In the first sentence the narrator seems to be describing a talus slope, not prevalent in the area. The configuration which puzzled him is due to glaciation.

[16] That is, in and to the west of Rosario or to the North of Cárdenas.

[17] The list has not been translated. For a more complete list of plants, with modern Latin and popular names, see Wilson, 1970. The rock specimens are not known to have been preserved, and are listed with identification numbers the author has been unable to trace.

reason we had been unable to notice any difference other than that of language, between the savages of the interior inlets and those of Nutca.[18]

Still, one language the navigators who had come to these shores could study was that of Nutca, finding this to extend from the entrance of Fuca to the Salida de las Goletas. It is to be noted that similarly the Nutqueños do not possess the language of their neighbours. For this [reason] the vocabulary which is placed at the end can be useful. It was formed during the time of our outpost, thanks for the most part to Don Pedro Alberni.[19]

The map which we present has all the accuracy permitted by the narrow inlets with precipitous sides, where astronomy with observations must supplement geodesy.[20] The artificial horizons had been in constant use, as much for latitudes as for longitudes by the chronometers, and after the longitude corresponding to the observation of the satellite of Jupiter at the anchorage at San Juan had been taken, all the longitudes on the coast had been corrected to the results of this observation, being preferable to all those made in this year and in the previous one during the expedition commanded by Don Alejandro Malaspina. The correction was applied to all the coast between San Blas and Nutca. In the part mapped by previous expeditions, we found the courses correct, even in detail, and only corrected the latitudes and longitudes. These last were defective because of the [available] means with which they had been established, distances having been overestimated. For the [actual longitude difference of] 1° 56' between Nutca and Nuñez Gaona they had estimated 2° 34'.[21]

---

[18] Much abbreviated in the *Viage*.

[19] The vocabulary is available in Wilson, 1970 and Kendrick, 1985, and has not been included in this volume.

[20] That is to say, the inlets were too crooked and steep to permit surveying during a limited season.

[21] In the *Viage*, an extensive section follows describing negotiations with Vancouver, which did not start until after Galiano had left Nootka. There is also a description of the fur trade, not based on the material in the manuscript.

XVI

The goletas depart from Nutca: The wind drives them offshore, and they cannot approach it [north of] 47 degrees of latitude: They explore the Entrada de Ezeta, and follow the coast until nearing the [points explored by] the corvettes: The weather again drives them away, and they do not sight land until [reaching] Cabo Mendocino: They cannot carry out the exploration until [reaching] Punta de Reyes, where they can again see the land, and they anchor in the Puerto de Monterey.

The settled favourable weather and our desire to examine the coast from the entry of Fuca to San Blas made us proceed actively [so that we would be able] to make our departure soon. On the 31st of August we exposed the bottoms of the goletas,[1] which were found to be free of damage. They were greased, with the intention of proceeding to sea during the night of this day with the land breeze.

We dined with the commandant Quadra, who with the utmost conscientiousness endeavoured to attend to the officers of the English ships, which conduct [Quadra] had [also] maintained with [the officers of] other foreign ships which had arrived at Nutca during his sojourn in that port. These had numbered sixteen, whom he had aided with food and with articles for their rigging.

---

[1] The *Viage* gives the same date, but Bodega y Quadra's journal says the goletas were heeled for inspection on September 1st.

At twelve at night we set sail,[2] having given to the English a copy of the part of our explorations which they selected, and having taken from them the portion of the north coast from Cabo Norte, with the adjacent islands, as well as the map of the shore of the entry of Fuca as far as 45° of latitude.[3] We left on a fresh north wind, the sky having cleared, but we soon lost it, and at daylight had not rounded the Punta de Arrecifes.[4]

The favourable appearance of the weather disappeared with the day, and during the night the wind had already settled in the east. This left us at sunset in sight of the coast of Nutca at 49° 13' of latitude, and 21° 34' of longitude west of San Blas.[5]

The wind continued from the east and southeast, obliging us to take the southern tack, which separated us from the coast. Our intention was to run along it all the way, and locate it from Fuca to Monterey, to which we were sailing, so we hardened up the sails as much as possible, so as not to be driven offshore. However, until the 4th, when at midday it started to slacken, the strong wind and sea opposed us so much that by then we were in 48° 20' of latitude and 21° 54' of longitude, and therefore forty leagues[6] from the coast.[7]

The wind backed to the first quadrant[8] and we sailed close hauled to sight land at the highest latitude permitted by the weather, but we did not attain this until the early hours of the 7th, in 47° of latitude, the weather being so clear that land could be made out at first light. In the interior a high mountain came

---

[2] This would have been the night of August 31st, according to the MS. However, this would mean that they left only ten hours after they arrived, having either heeled or careened the ships, and having greased their bottoms. Bodega y Quadra's journal says they left at daylight on the 2nd, and the extract of the journal sent from Monterey says that they left at one in the morning of September 2nd. It seems likely that they left during the night of September 1st - September 2nd.

[3] That is to say, of Puget Sound, which none of the Spanish explorers had entered.

[4] Only the last sentence is in the *Viage*.

[5] [Footnote in the MS.] The meridian of San Blas is considered to be 99° 5' west of Cádiz, and longitudes which follow are referred to San Blas.

[6] About 220 km.   [7] This paragraph is shortened in the *Viage*.

[8] Between east and north.

in view to the southeast with a flat summit, and to the northeast a range of mountains with sharp peaks, with low lying land between them. The whole coast had a low beach at the [edge of the] sea.[9]

But with the rising of the sun fog set in and obscured our sight of the land. We approached it, sounding line in hand, until the noise of the surf warned us of its proximity. We arrived in this situation at ten thirty in the morning, and in a depth of 16 fathoms fine grey sand. We steered SE 1/4 S, and sailed on soundings, within earshot of the surf, keeping to a depth of 14 to 18 fathoms, with the same bottom.

From the 4th, the wind had been weak from a generally northerly direction, and in our present position it blew light from the NW. After midday it cleared somewhat, and we could take a bearing on a low point at S 56° E, but the fog returned, so dense that the goletas could not see each other, and maintained contact with the sound of shots from the small swivel gun.[10] In this situation, the wind went round to the west and started to freshen, placing us in quite a critical situation, since we found ourselves on a coast without harbours, inhabited by Indians who had proved their ferocity by assassinating seven seamen of the launch of the schooner *Sonora*,[11] completely fogged in, with a rising onshore wind, and in two ships which were not adapted for getting free of [the shore.] We adopted the course of sailing close hauled under the driver, topsail, foresail and foretopsail,[12] pointing the prow to the S 1/4 SW. Fortunately, the wind dropped three hours later, returning to the NW; the sky cleared, and the land became visible, towards which we immediately steered. Our desire to examine it was so strong that we gave in only to immediate adverse weather. With other normal ships we would not have been driven off so far, nor would we have lost so

---

[9] The *Viage* says only that they approached the land in 47° latitude.

[10] Esmeril.

[11] This had happened in 1775, somewhat to the north of the place where the goletas were at this time.

[12] Por los cuatro principales.

much latitude, but our circumstances obliged us not to risk ourselves with an imprudence as inexcusable as [it would have been] probably useless. [13]

The land which we caught sight of was a large bay, which extends from the Punta Gorda as far as San Cayetano. In between there is a harbour explored by the English Captain Gray, [14] with little water [depth] in the entry, of which the Commandant Quadra had given us a plan. Nightfall prevented our exploring it. It was calm, and we passed the night lying to, standing on and off, so as not to go by the Entrada de Ezeta. [15]

At daylight on the 8th of September we were off a coast with a cape to the SE, which we supposed to be San Roque, north of the entry seen by Don Bruno de Ezeta in 1775. This point was one of the most important of our commission, since it had not been seen after that time by [our explorers.] Neither had the English seen such an entry during their explorations. The Commandant Vancouver, who had closely examined the coast, said that no important entry could exist on the whole coast from 45° to the entry of Fuca. We wished to put such trustworthy information in order, and for this reason we had taken care to spare no risk to verify it. Fresh winds, in which regular ships could sail with all plain sail, would push the goletas three or four points off course in going one or two miles. Any sailor who might know this would come to understand the risks in which the goletas were off the coast. [16]

We directed ourselves towards the cape in 13 fathoms of water, but as soon as we drew near, the depth greatly decreased.

---

[13] This and the previous paragraph are omitted from the *Viage*.

[14] Robert Gray, an American then commanding the *Columbia*. The bay is Gray's Harbour.

[15] The mouth of the Columbia River, sighted by Hezeta [Ezeta] but named for Gray's ship.

[16] This paragraph seems to be a justification of the failure of the goletas to carry out their instructions. It is, understandably, shortened in the *Viage*.

We passed the cape close by in 3 fathoms sand, and as soon as we cleared it, a bay presented itself with an entry at its end three miles wide. The turbid colour of the water, its small depth, and its turbulence left us no doubt that we found ourselves at the mouth of a river. The Commandant Quadra had given us a plan of an exploration by the English ship *Columbia*,[17] which we compared to what we saw. We continued sailing in 3 to 5 fathoms, and as soon as we were somewhat clear of Cabo de San Roque to the south, we realized that it was the very Entrada de Ezeta, because the cape appeared to be an island.[18] The land at the end of the bay between [Cabo San Roque] and Cabo Falcon is very low.[19] We were therefore convinced that the reason it had been considered a large entry was that it had been seen from a great distance, and the error in latitude which contradicts this idea arises from not having taken an observation close by to establish it.[20]

Our ships were not of a type to encourage us to stay on the coast longer than the exact time required to fix the location of prominent points, and so we followed the coast closely. During this day, we obtained the first benefit [contributing] to the purpose we had since leaving Nutca, the plotting of the part of the coast from 46° 8' to 46° 35'.

The next day, although the wind shifted between northwest and west, it was steady, which with the clear sky offered us the same good fortune.[21] We saw the Cabo de Maltiempo, named by the celebrated Cook for the strong tempest experienced there

[17] Gray's [American] ship; see above.

[18] Hezeta's map shows the high ground of Cape Disappointment including North Head as an island.

[19] The cape that Galiano took to be Cabo Falcon must be Tillamook Head. South of this point, a series of cliffs and high rocky bluffs rises from the shoreline. Hezeta named Cabo Falcon in 1775; the difference in latitude from Cabo San Roque as quoted in his journal suggests that Hezeta and Galiano were talking of the same cape. The present Cape Falcon is further south. Beals, 1985 cites different opinions on this point

[20] In the *Viage*, the last sentence is omitted, and estimates of latitude and longitude are added. This change was not made by Galiano when he was editing the journal in Madrid.

[21] Sentence omitted from the *Viage*.

on his second voyage of exploration,[22] and to the south of it a small opening was seen towards which we steered under full sail. On drawing near we saw that a heavy sea was set up directly at the entrance. We arrived at a depth of 7 fathoms, sand bottom, and at two lengths of the goletas [from the entry] the seas broke. We saw that the entry was narrow, that the sea stretched inland, and that there were some huts and inhabitants, but that it was not feasible for ships to enter.[23]

We followed the coast to the south, and saw two more small openings of the same type as the first. All the coast [we] explored was of medium height, its beaches shelving, and covered with pines and mangroves,[24] but in the interior various mountains rose, forming a range of medium height. Only to the northeast of the Entrada de Ezeta did a steep ridge covered with snow come in sight, which could be the source of the Columbia River, or at least greatly augment its flow. At nightfall the wind dropped, and by ten we were in a flat calm broken only by a steady light swell from the west, which we had noticed for three days.[25]

Thus it continued in the morning, and we could not make running fixes. The sky clouded over and in the night the land breeze rose, which filled in so that at eight in the morning it was a fresh breeze, which strengthened to the point that it obliged us to lie to,[26] under reefed mainsail. We were forced away from the coast, which was already out of sight at daybreak. After two days it cleared, but the wind being settled in the SE, alternating with calms and southerly winds, set us away from the coast as far as fifty leagues. Fortunately we had reached the part seen during the previous year by the corvettes, and this made its exploration

---

[22] In fact, Cook named Cape Foulweather on his third voyage.

[23] This was Yaquina Bay.

[24] The coast of Oregon and northern California do not have mangrove swamps. The nature of this vegetation is uncertain.

[25] Paragraph omitted from the *Viage*.

[26] Set a few sails in such a way that the vessel lay in the trough of the sea, making little progress. The Spanish verb is "capear."

less important.[27] As soon as the winds got into the third quadrant[28] we sailed close hauled in the second quadrant, with the intention of returning to the coast. On the 19th the wind changed to the fourth quadrant, and on the morning of the 20th we could catch sight of land near Cabo Mendocino. This is quite high, and appears to be formed by the mountains which follow the coast as far as the eye could see. We were going to follow it from this cape to Punta de Reyes, when the wind freshened from the NW, with gathering storm clouds and increased strength. We had no alternative but to run off, hauling taut the foresail and main topsail so the goletas would not be pooped by the following sea. We went along thus until the afternoon of the 21st, when we saw the Farallones de San Francisco.[29] It took until the 23rd to anchor at Monterey, the weather having been adverse for all but two days that could be said to have been favourable for our purpose.[30]

---

[27] Most of this paragraph is omitted from the *Viage*.

[28] To the west of south.

[29] The word "farallon" means a high rocky spire, either on a point of land or as an isolated rock in the sea. It is used in the latter sense in the manuscript.

[30] The *Viage* just says they sighted Mendocino on the 20th and anchored at Monterey on the 23rd.

XVII

The frigate Santa Gertrudis *is met in Monterey: Our crew takes some rest, and the inlets [we had] explored are mapped: The brig* Activa *and the sloop* Bentura *arrive: The Commandant Quadra orders the schooner* Saturnina *to go to the Puerto de San Francisco: The frigate* Aránzazu *arrives and the sloop* Bentura *is despatched to Nutca.*

Anchored in the harbour was the frigate *Santa Gertrudis*, commanded by Don Alonso de Torres, which had left the Puerto de Núñez Gaona on the 26th of July, and arrived on 11th August, without having been able to achieve any examination anywhere on the coast other than the entry of Ezeta, at a long distance, having been thwarted by the weather, and being short of food, for which reason they had not waited [longer] in hope of an opportune occasion.

The Puerto de Monterey offers a very good haven for the rest and refreshment of the crew. Ours, although in the best of health, were tired from their continuous labours and the cramped space in the ships, and looked at the harbour with all the pleasure that could be imagined. At this time they considered they were free of danger, which they could have come across in the high latitudes, and free of the dismay which they felt on their departure from San Blas and Acapulco, in which harbours there had been an unfortunate announcement of the campaign of the goletas. They were given the liberty deserved by their work, to which they responded with honour and good conduct. [1]

We used the time of our stay at Monterey to plot the map of our explorations made from our departure from Nutca [in June] until our return to that harbour. The lack of space in the ships had not permitted it to be drawn, and we had been reduced to accumulating the notes with the greatest clarity, to combine and extend them at an appropriate opportunity. A room ashore offered this, and by the 24th October[2] we had already calculated and laid down the most important of our observations in that region.[3]

On the 9th of October the brig *Activa* came in, with the sloop *Bentura*,[4] after nineteen days of sailing from the Puerto de Nutca, where the corvette *Aránzazu* had remained under the command of Ship Lieutenant Don Jacinto Caamaño, after having carried out its commission to complete the exploration of the Puerto de Bucareli, and making various other [explorations] along the coast to the south of it. They travelled between the coast and various islands, discovering a wide inlet, and making the most of the means at their disposal. Caamaño waited for the arrival at Nutca of Lieutenant Don Salvador Fidalgo in the frigate *Princesa*, to replace him, and to maintain this establishment for us until the Courts of Spain and England should decide whether we must deliver the Puerto de Nutca to the English, or only the parcels of land and buildings of which they had been dispossessed in 1789. Captain Vancouver had remained with his ships in that harbour to await the best lunar

---

[1] This sentence omitted from the *Viage*.

[2] The *Viage* gives the date as 20th October, but the 24th is retained in MS 1060, as amended by Galiano in 1794-5.

[3] The rest of this chapter is omitted from the *Viage*. In its place are sailing directions for the approach to Monterey, followed by a lengthy description of that place and its indigenous people, the latter taken from Venegas.

[4] This sloop, originally named *Adventure*, was built by Gray at Nootka in the winter of 1791-2. In September, 1792, he traded it to Bodega y Quadra for sea otter skins. It was renamed *Horcasitas*, one of the many names of Viceroy Revillagigedo, but Galiano is using the old name. See: Bodega y Quadra, 1792.

distances available to him, because he had noted in those he had then taken a considerable difference from those indicated by Captain Cook.

During our exploration in the corvettes, we could count on a degree of accuracy in longitude which few navigators had been able to attain[5] by our use of different astronomical observations and continual checking of the chronometers ashore. On one occasion we had found a difference of three quarters of a degree from the true longitude. There were many observations, repeated in series over an interval of four days, giving this constant error. This indicates that it can be attributed almost entirely to an error in the tables with which the distances were computed. Thus, far from agreeing that longitude by lunar distances can be relied on to a quarter of a degree as had been advanced by some, one should only rely on them to the said three quarters, accepting that in most cases the mean of various series could be within one quarter of a degree. So we told Captain Vancouver, to whom our proposition was strange because of the ideas established in England by the best astronomers, who had predetermined, as an exact method of establishing longitude, the mean of many lunar distances.

On the 13th the schooner *Saturnina* arrived, commanded by Master's Mate[6] Don Juan Carrasco, who had left San Blas on the 10th of June to take sealed orders to Don Juan de la Quadra at Nutca. This ship, although shorter in the keel than ours, was better designed and in consequence safer at sea, but facing adverse winds, they could not go beyond 42° of latitude because of a shortage of supplies.[7] After having used all the steadfastness of [which] Carrasco and his crew [were capable], it was seen to be necessary to go to the Puerto de San Francisco to revictual

---

[5] Malaspina's longitude estimate for Nutca is only three minutes off. Vancouver's was eight minutes off, still a creditable performance.

[6] Pilotin.

[7] Carrasco did not have such a good opinion of his vessel. He reported that his failure to get to Nootka was because of the bad sailing qualities of his ship. AGN Historia 67.

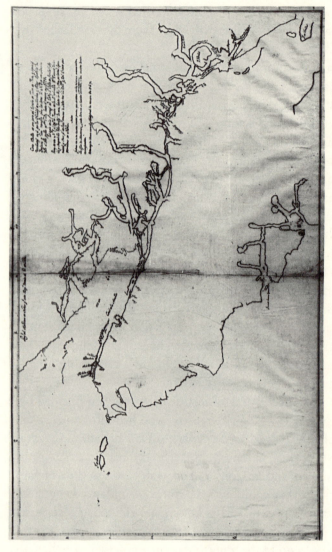

Galiano's map of his explorations. The maps started as rough sketches and notes made in the ships' boats while they were under way, then progressed through various stages to a final version for engraving. This is an early draft of the complete map.

Courtesy of Museo Naval, Madrid.

and then continue the task. However, the Commandant of the frigate *Gertrudis* had turned him back, and as soon as he arrived at San Blas the Commandant there gave him the order to proceed to Monterey.

On the 22nd the corvette *Aránzazu* arrived, leaving at Nutca the mentioned *Princesa*, which had come from Fuca with its Commandant[8] to occupy the harbour until further orders.

The order of the Court, which Carrasco brought to Quadra, instructed him to send the sloop *Bentura* to Nutca with orders for that establishment. For this he asked our help with food, and we were able to aid him with some bread and ham, the first of which had stayed [in] excellent [condition] because of the good order in which we had placed the lockers.

The sloop sailed on the 22nd for its voyage. This vessel, although of a shorter keel than the goletas, had an appropriate beam, with regular sails, and was no worse than other small ships. Its cabins and accommodation for the crew were spacious and comfortable.

---

[8] Fidalgo.

XVIII

The goletas leave Monterey, and because of bad weather fail to explore the coast until [reaching] the Canal de Santa Bárbara: They explore the islands which form it, Mexicana *passing to the north and* Sutil *to the south of them; They enter the Puerto de San Diego, where they see the corvette* Concepción *anchored; They follow the coast as far as 27° 30' of latitude, and leave it to explore the Farallones de Alixos: They arrive at Cabo de San Lucas: The corvette* Concepción *joins them, and they sight the Islas Marías: A strong gale off [the islands] and danger to the goletas: In the end, they successfully come to anchor in the Puerto de San Blas.*

On the 23rd [of October][1] we were ready to set sail for San Blas, but the wind strengthened from the north, and neither we nor the frigate *Gertrudis* could achieve this. We sent the map we had made to the Viceroy of New Spain by the frigate, with an extract of the journal of our explorations.[2] On the 25th the weather moderated, and at two in the morning of the 26th we weighed, leaving the frigate behind.[3]

At daylight we had already cleared the Punta de Pinos, but the strong gusty southeast wind which blew during the day was adverse for following the coast, and separated us from it, so that it was out of sight at sunset. The following night was stormy, with a heavy rain squall at one thirty which was the end of the southeaster. The sky cleared in the northwest and clear indica-

---

[1] The *Viage* gives the date as the 22nd.

[2] This is in the AGN in Mexico, under Provincias Internas 134. It is a summary of the material in Chapters IV to XVI in this work.

[3] Abbreviated in the *Viage*.

tions were seen of a wind from this direction. It was not long in coming, and we had good weather all day on the 27th, making use of it to set a course for the Canal de Santa Bárbara.[4]

This channel, formed by the coast and a range of islands, had to be examined because during the previous year the corvettes had located some points on the principal islands, and they differed so much from the maps [then] used for navigation that the course of the channel could not be reconciled without arbitrarily changing the position of [some of] the islands which had not been seen. In consequence one of the principal objectives of our commission was to examine it.[5] In view of the season and the type of ships we had, such a course was risky in the judgement of the Commandant Quadra and of his coastal pilots trained on this route. Since there are no harbours to provide shelter from the south winds which come with violence and bad visibility, they advised us not to undertake it.[6]

On the 28th, at midday we saw the [bordering] lands, and made for the channel. At nightfall, it being close by, it was decided to separate the goletas, to make a map of the most important and least explored islands. This was because the ships which transit the channel always go by the coast, to deliver stores to the missions which are [situated] in it. *Mexicana* steered to pass along the north shore of the islands, and *Sutil* along the south shore, to rejoin off the Isla de Catalina.[7]

On the 29th at ten thirty in the morning, the Farallones de Lobos were sighted. During this day we ran along the Islas de San Cleto[8] and San Miguel, shortening sail at night.[9] With a

---

[4] This paragraph omitted from the *Viage*.

[5] This is an exaggeration, but such an examination was desired by Malaspina. See the Introduction.

[6] Paragraph omitted from the *Viage*.

[7] This paragraph is omitted from the *Viage*.

[8] A mistranscription for an abbreviated form of San Clemente. Further mistranscribed as "Anacleto" in the *Viage*.

[9] The identity of these islands is uncertain. There are four islands in the northern group now known as the Channel Islands, of which Galiano mentions only two. They were renamed so often prior to 1800 that not even Wagner [1937] produced a satisfactory identification of all the names. The map included in the *Viage* shows four islands, but it is based on explorations "in 1791 and 1792 by the goletas *Sutil* and *Mexicana* and other of His Majesty's ships."

very bright moon we explored the island of Santa Bárbara, making a running fix in sight of it, and taking the meridian altitude of the moon along the base.[10]

At daylight on the 31st we were off the northwest point of the Isla de Santa Catalina, at which place the goletas reunited, making running fixes on the south part of this island, succeeding by afternoon in being at its southeast extremity, from where we determined geometrically the boundaries of the Isla de San Andrés.[11] Since it was far off, for the accuracy of the bearings, the precaution was taken to make use of the sun, determining bearings without the compass, by the azimuths of this celestial body and the vertical angle it formed with the points we located.[12]

We passed a calm night, and at daybreak [on 1st November] were off the Isla de San Andrés. We had light airs during the day, which did not afford an opportunity for drawing a rough plan of this island. The next day was the same. We made use of the best of the light airs to make for the Puerto de San Diego, having by then located all the islands. Even though we had no more than one bearing on San Nicolas, it had already been located by the goletas in the previous year.[13] These islands are of medium height and have no tree cover. Among them only Santa Catalina affords two harbours, in the middle of its northeast and southwest coastlines, separated by a league of narrow low land.[14]

The fine weather which had favoured our passage of the channel took on the worst aspect during the night. We stayed in sight of the coast, and there a violent storm built up, with a southwest wind and heavy rain, but it dropped in a few hours,

---

[10] The lunar altitude, in conjunction with other data on the ship's position, would fix approximately the position of the object on the map. This and the following paragraph are shortened in the *Viage*.

[11] The present San Clemente, which name is used in the *Viage*.

[12] They were making use of the altitudes and directions of the sun, calculated from astronomical tables, rather than relying on the compass. In view of the approximations in calculating distances and the uncertainty of the ship's position, the precision of this method is illusory.

[13] The *Viage* reads "by the corvettes," which is probably correct. *Sutil* and *Mexicana* had not been at sea in 1791, and there is no other pair of "goletas."

[14] Shortened in the *Viage*.

and by morning it was gentle. It settled in the west, the sky cleared, and we steered for the Punta de San Diego, the latitude and longitude of which we were working to determine. We passed close to it, sounding at the edge of the weeds, and giving sea room to the shoal which stretches out to the south of the point. As soon as we rounded this, we sighted the frigate *Concepción* which we had left in Nutca on our departure for the exploration of Fuca. A pinnace came off with Ship Ensign Don Juan Matute, who informed us that the corvette[15] had been detained by a lack of provisions for its voyage to San Blas, which it was replenishing.

We entered the bay, skirting the west shore because there are shallows on the east side, which reach beyond mid channel, making the entrance to the harbour difficult. It was our aim to be due east of the Punta de San Diego at midday to determine its latitude, and accordingly we turned from [a point] near the entrance of the harbour, and carried out the observation of the meridian altitude of the sun satisfactorily.

We followed the shore, the pinnace returning to the harbour. The wind was fresh and the weather continued pleasant, permitting us to use the pass between the Coronados and the shore, and to make a plan of that part of the shore between which lies between the Punta de San Diego and latitude 32° 10′.

Since our operations could not be directed to do more than to locate the shore, which remained sufficiently close to its position [on previous maps], we stayed on course carrying out what work the day permitted. We continued our operations under this policy. On the 4th we covered the part from 31° 35′ to 31° 20′; on the 5th from 30° 30′ as far as 29° 45′; on the 6th the part of the Golfo de Cerros[16] from 15° 45′ of longitude to 14° 45′; on the 7th we continued along the

---

[15] This must mean *Concepción*. The designations "frigate" and "corvette" were used indiscriminately.

[16] The southern part of this is now the Bahía de Sebastián Vizcaíno. The account of this differs in the *Viage*.

east side of the Isla de Cerros, travelling by the narrows between the Isla Trinidad and the shore, which ends in 27° 30' of latitude in a bay with good holding ground in sand, which could be the Puerto de San Bartolomé, so named by Sebastián Vizcaíno.[17]

We would have followed the shore as far as Cabo de San Lucas if our attention had not been drawn to another more important point. The maps of the pilots of the Department of San Blas placed some rocky islands called the Alijos in 24° of latitude, but on its return voyage to Acapulco in 1792[18] the frigate *San Andrés* of the Phillipines trade, had made an observation in the latitude [of Alijos] of 23° 34', recording its work with a certainty and individuality, which obliged Ship Captain Malaspina to give it consideration, and to place on his map this last position as being preferable.[19] The pilots had established their [positions], and in view of their journals and the strong reasons on which the [positions] were founded, this point merited our preferential examination.

In consequence we set our course to reach the parallel of the Alixos twenty leagues to the west, where we arrived at four in the afternoon of the 9th.[20] At this point a second separation of the goletas was decided on, with *Mexicana* running along the parallel of 24° 56' and *Sutil* that of 24° 30', thus leaving an interval of 36 [sic] miles,[21] and hoping in this way to explore all the latitudes in which the Alixos might lie. After comparing the chronometers, we set our rendezvous at 24° 30' of latitude and 15° of longitude.[22]

We did not want to sail more than twelve miles during the

---

[17] Vizcaíno was a Spanish captain who explored the west coasts of Mexico and Baja California around the end of the sixteenth century.

[18] This must have been 1791.

[19] The reference to Malaspina is deleted from the *Viage*.

[20] The manuscript gives the date as the 19th, in figures, but this must be wrong.

[21] This should read 26 miles if the latitudes are correct. The same error appears in AGN Hist. 558. The latitudes given here are inconsistent with those given in the previous paragraph, which appear to be wrongly stated, judging by subsequent paragraphs.

[22] Fifteen degrees west of San Blas would be far to seaward of the Alijos Rocks. This must be west of Acapulco.

night which would overrun the part we had seen [before night-fall], therefore we stood on and off until daylight [on November 11th], then ran down our parallel to the east.

But much to our surprise we found by our noon observation that we had lost ten minutes [of latitude] to the south, even considering that on our tacks during the night under courses we had done no more than to maintain our position, and that during the previous days we had experienced no current. When the loss [of latitude] became known, *Sutil* started to sail into the wind with a full spread of sail but the next day we found ourselves in 24° 22′ having lost 40″ more than the 21′ we had gained according to the dead reckoning.[23]

Mexicana, which had the same loss [of latitude] fell down to 24° 30′ and their forces being ineffective in returning them to [the prescribed] latitude, its commander decided to follow that [assigned to] *Sutil*, considering that a similar event would have happened to this vessel. The parallel of 24° 34′ was examined satisfactorily, *Mexicana* in 24° 38′ and *Sutil* in 24° 30′, and on the 13th at two in the morning, the goletas rejoined at the agreed latitude and longitude. In this occurrence[24] the bad sailing properties of the goletas were also an obstacle, but we could be sure that the Alixos were not in the position given by the frigate *San Andrés*, nor within 20′ of it, and consequently that the position given by the pilots was the reliable one. The corvette *Concepción*, which left the harbour of San Diego, and made for them, sighted them, correcting the latitude and longitude in which they had been located.[25]

The goletas having rejoined company, they set a course for the Cabo de San Lucas. The wind continued fresh from the

[23] The figures in this paragraph appear to mean that the noon observation placed them in latitude 24° 20′, rather than the planned 24° 30′. They then tried to beat to the northward, but the current set them back almost the full 22 miles that they had travelled through the water, according to their dead reckoning. The editor of the *Viage* changed the sense of the whole paragraph.

[24] The set to the south which they could not overcome.

[25] The Alijos Rocks are in latitude 24° 55′.

WNW and the weather clear, and hence at daylight on the 15th, the coast line of the extreme south of the Peninsula de las Californias was sighted, and at noon we were in the meridian of Cabo San Lucas. Using it as a base, we took hour angles at its end, and found that the chronometer Arnold 344 gave 13' less of a difference between it and Monterey than had been established in the corvettes during the previous year. During our campaign we had gained little profit from chronometer number 16,[26] so we conceded that the results from a single chronometer [were less reliable than] those that had been determined by many better ones [in the corvettes] and corrected our intermediate longitudes, allowing an arithmetic progression of the error of the chronometer, finding this assumption confirmed when the chronometer was checked in San Blas.[27]

We still had to examine the Islas Marías and Isla Ysabela, before arriving at our destination. There had been some dispute over their position, the pilots of the Department of San Blas having advanced some reasons against the position in which they had been placed by the corvettes. We had to confirm these points. Three days of good winds would have been sufficient for this objective, but in crossing the mouth of the Mar de Cortes we had calm winds and tranquil seas, and we started to lose way. On the 18th a ship was sighted to the west and at midday it had joined us. It was the corvette *Concepción*, under the command of Ship Lieutenant Don Francisco de Elisa. He paid us the courtesy of joining us, shortening sail, because his ship greatly had the advantage of us. We continued in convoy, taking advantage of the fair winds which freshened on the 20th in the afternoon,

---

[26] This should be number 61, see Chapter VII. The instrument is listed in the equipment aboard Malaspina's ships. See Higueras, 1987.

[27] An observation of hour angles can be used in one of two ways. If the time is known, the observation will give the longitude. If the longitude is known, it will give the correct local time. Because the timepieces in the corvettes were considered more reliable than those in the goletas, the latter option was chosen, and proven correct when they reached San Blas, where the longitude was well known. This paragraph is shortened in the *Viage*.

putting us in a position to see the most northwesterly of the Marías at nightfall from the mastheads of the *Concepción*.

On the 21st we reached them by daylight, observing the latitude of the most northerly point, and we could make no further progress in mapping them because calms supervened. At nightfall we followed along them. The sky was threatening and the current set us to the southeast, pushing us towards the narrows between the two northerly Marías.[28]

At one in the morning [of 22nd November] a storm wind came up which placed us at some risk. It started as a northerly, and backed to the west. There was such a blast of wind that although *Mexicana* took it with the main slacked away it almost capsized. *Sutil* placed itself astern with topsails eased,[29] but what gave the greatest concern was that with the strong wind and rain the binnacle lights were extinguished, principally because the glasses had been broken. The spare lantern kept for this purpose was put in use, but it too was extinguished, and left the goletas without knowing what course they were steering. We anxiously awaited the illumination of the lightning flashes to see the compass and get free both of the islands and of the corvette *Concepción*. The strength of the wind dropped as we left the islands, affording us easy seas, but the goletas had not come in sight of each other all night, the first time they had lost touch with the exception of the two occasions on which they had [separated] purposely. In spite of the small object they presented [to the view] close co-operation and care had avoided any separation.

At daybreak the goletas were reunited, and they asked the commander of the *Concepción* to sail on to the harbour, recognizing that the delay he was accepting did not result in any advantage. He immediately made full sail and placed his ship on course.

[28] Shortened in the *Viage*.

[29] Under bare poles, according to the *Viage*.

After taking bearings on the Marías, we made for Ysabela to continue our work. The squally weather and gusty wind prevented our achieving the desired accuracy. Although we could not observe the latitude at noon we calculated it from two altitudes of the sun. This proved to us the great distance to the south that we had been carried by the current. In the afternoon the wind freshened from the southeast and the sky cleared somewhat. We saw Ysabela and steered for it. We made a running fix, at the same time taking bearings on the Marías and the Cerro de San Juan.[30]

It was squally at nightfall, with *Concepción* in sight. During the night, after a squall with considerable rain and wind, the sky cleared, the wind shifted to WNW, and we steered to find the white rock by which the harbour can be recognized. At dawn it was in sight, also *Concepción* a long way off astern. We anchored at eleven in the morning [of 23rd November], finding in the harbour the frigate of war *Gertrudis*, and the corvette *San José y las Animas*, which had arrived from Manila under the command of Frigate Lieutenant Don Manuel Quimper.[31]

Our crew arrived in the best of health and happiness, receiving the congratulations of their friends on seeing them free from such a risky and laborious voyage on which they had given proof of an obedience and steadfastness worthy of the highest praise.[32]

Mexico, the 18th of October, 1793.

[signed] DIONISIO ALCALÁ GALIANO

---

[30] A mountain east of San Blas.

[31] This and the previous paragraph are omitted from the *Viage*.

[32] The *Viage* adds a further paragraph.

DRAMATIS PERSONAE

The five protagonists of our story probably did not see it as a drama. Hardship and danger were not new to a sailor, and there is no trace in the documents of the wonder of discovery, the fascination of encounters with the strange Indian people, or the excitement of meeting the English explorers in the remote waters of "Fuca."

Still less would these five have seen themselves as actors in a drama. They were living normal naval lives, trying to achieve promotion or to wangle allowances to supplement their pay, arguing for the advancement of subordinates who had done well, and submitting endless and sometimes hopeless lists of things they needed. To them, the voyage of *Sutil* and *Mexicana* was an incident in a long career: an unusual one, but an incident all the same. To us, the voyage is the origin of our knowledge of part of the coast of British Columbia and some of its inhabitants.

In the papers dealing with the voyage and the records of their service, we get an occasional glimpse of the characters of the people, but that is all. We get more glimpses in unnumbered dossiers maintained by the Museo Naval for many officers. While these lack the precision of official service records, they contain correspondence and petitions lacking from the official record, such as a petition by a widow of Alicante for permission to marry Valdés without losing her pension, and attempts by the father of Juan Vernacci to speed up his son's promotion. In Galiano's case, these are supplemented by Salvá, and by the *Enciclopedia General del Mar*. For Cardero, the biography in

Sotos, Volume I, has been consulted, together with documents of the Malaspina voyage.

The lives of all five explorers, possibly excepting Vernacci's, became directly involved in the drama that was the history of Spain during their lifetimes. They left Cádiz in Malaspina's ships at the time of the fall of the Bastille in Paris, and just as Carlos IV in Madrid was beginning to weed out his father's advisers and to install his own favourites in various offices of State.

War and peace alternated during the years after their return, leading to the naval battle off Trafalgar in October 1805 in which the British defeated the combined fleets of Spain and France. Carlos IV invited Napoleon to send an army through Spain to attack Britain's ally, Portugal, but it was soon discovered that the French had occupied the principal strategic bases in Spain. After more turmoil, Carlos IV relinquished the Spanish throne to the French, and Napoleon installed his brother Joseph Bonaparte as King of Spain in 1808. This brought about a broadly based but almost leaderless resistance to the French, engendered by a profound sense of national pride, and by the danger to the privileges of the landowning class. The resistance included regular army formations, but its main strength, which persisted until the defeat and withdrawal of the Napoleonic forces, was in the guerilla bands who harassed the French everywhere in Spain. The British, who were protecting their ally Portugal, eventually entered the fray. The Spanish resistance had coalesced around a General Council, which proclaimed a liberal constitution in 1812, and had a measure of control in part of Spain from then on. In 1813 the Napoleonic forces were finally defeated by Wellington, with the aid of the supporters of the Spanish resistance. The General Council recalled Fernando VII, the son of Carlos IV, to the throne he had briefly occupied in 1808.

The resistance forces had high hopes of Fernando VII, but

they were soon disillusioned. Absolutist government returned to Spain in 1814, the Council was dissolved, and liberals were exiled or removed from their posts. By this time, most of the American colonies were in revolt, and the Spanish Empire was collapsing. In 1820 the 1812 constitution was reintroduced, and the liberals came back, or at least some of them. The Cortes, a body consisting of the Senate and Congress, gained effective if temporary control. In 1823, Fernando was deposed for a short time, and a Regency appointed by the Cortes took over. However, with French support, Fernando soon regained power, and maintained it until his death in 1833. The regency that was established after his death granted amnesty to the liberals in 1834.

The Carlist wars followed, but by that time our protagonists were either dead or too old to take part.

DIONISIO ALCALA GALIANO sometimes signed his full surname as Alcalá-Galiano, which would have been correct, but in the correspondence mentioning his name, as well as in the journal of the 1792 voyage he was referred to as "Galiano." That is the reason he is so called in this book.

Galiano was born in Cabra, in Córdoba province, on October 8, 1760. On proof of his patent of nobility and his legitimate birth, he was accepted into the Guardia Marina, we would say as a midshipman, in 1775. His first promotion came within three years, during which interval he spent most of his time on convoy duty in the South Atlantic. He studied astronomy, and got his reward in 1783 when he was assigned to work under the great hydrographer and mathematician Vicente Tofiño, who was engaged in making a map of the coastline of Spain.

In 1785, Galiano was a Frigate Lieutenant. There is a record of his marriage in that year to María de la Consolación Villavicencio. Presumably the anchorage of Villavicencio (see Chapter XIV) was named in her honour, but it is one of the Spanish place names that has disappeared from the maps.

Soon after his marriage, Galiano left on a survey of the Strait of Magellan under the command of Antonio de Córdoba. Sudden gales cost them four anchors, and the progress of the survey was extremely slow. They were away for eight months, and arrived back in Cádiz with some of the crew suffering from scurvy, and exhausted from battling against storms on the way.

Galiano had command of the brig *Natalia* in 1788, on a mission to fix the location of the Azores. By that time he was a Ship Lieutenant. After his return, he worked on a survey of the harbour of Cádiz, then in December 1788 he was appointed to the Malaspina expedition, sailing with Bustamante in *Atrevida*. It was a late appointment, made to replace another officer who had previously been selected.

During the year and a half the Malaspina expedition spent mapping the coast of South America, and examining the flora and fauna inland, Galiano made full use of his hydrographic training under Tofiño and Córdoba. He carried out many astronomic observations during the voyage, as well as gravitational and magnetic measurements. His work during the *Sutil* voyage, then while he was in Mexico in 1792-3, and later with Malaspina in Madrid has already been described. He had been promoted to Frigate Captain on March 1, 1791, and to Ship Captain on his return to Spain, effective January 25, 1794. After Malaspina's arrest, Galiano worked on a new topographic map of Spain until 1796, when he returned to sea. The map seems not to have been completed.

He commanded a ship in the Cape St. Vincent battle in 1797, and in 1798 he was given command of the light squadron protecting the port of Cádiz. Next, he went with a group of ships to the Caribbean to bring treasure to Spain. Galiano had to slip out of Cádiz past the British blockade. He did it at night during a storm, sailed to the Caribbean, and picked up silver and other valuables at Cartagena (Colombia) and Veracruz. He had to evade enemy ships a number of times on his way home, but got back safely to Cádiz with the Royal treasure. He made a second treasure voyage to New Spain, commanding a small squadron coming back. British ships and bad weather drove him into Havana, where he was when the Peace of Amiens ended the war in 1802.

He was promoted to Brigadier (Commodore) in that year, and served mainly in the Mediterranean for three years, carrying out such commissions as mapping the eastern part of that sea, and bringing the chosen bride of the future King Fernando VII to Spain from Naples.

In December 1804 the Treaty of Amiens disintegrated, and Spain was again at war with England. Galiano was given command of *Bahama*, a seventy-six-gun ship. He was killed at Trafalgar, on October 21, 1805, and buried at sea, from his half wrecked ship.

Galiano's widow was awarded a pension, but it all went to pay her late husband's debts. His son Antonio became a liberal politician and writer, whose book "Recollections of an Old Man" is one of the important historic documents of his time.

CAYETANO VALDES Y FLORES was born in Sevilla in 1767. He was a nephew of Antonio Valdés, for many years the Minister of the Navy. He was accepted into the company of midshipmen, (Guardia Marina) before his fourteenth birthday. Eighteen months later he was raised to the rank of Alférez de Fragata, and was on his way to quick promotion as a naval officer. By that time, he had already been in action against the English fleet under Howe, off Gibraltar.

Valdés was promoted to Frigate Lieutenant in 1785, several months before his eighteenth birthday. His family connections may have influenced his rapid promotion, but his later career, especially after his uncle retired in 1796, indicates that his own merits had a lot to do with it.

His next promotion, to Ship Lieutenant, came three years later, on his selection to join the Malaspina expedition as an officer in *Descubierta*. At that time he was equal in rank to Galiano, but with a year's less seniority. On March 1, 1791, when *Descubierta* was mapping the west coast of Mexico, both Valdés and Galiano were promoted to the rank of Frigate Captain. From that date until Galiano's death, they always held equal rank with the same seniority, both ascending to the rank of Brigadier on October 5, 1802.

Valdés was wounded at Trafalgar, but recovered. After the battle, he was promoted to Gefe de Escuadra (Rear Admiral). He was given the command of the Cartagena squadron (the Mediterranean Fleet) in 1807. The upheavals in Madrid caught up with him soon after. He was removed from his post to make way for an officer acceptable to the French, but was soon restored to his command. The war was so fluid that Valdés led a division of the army for a time, being gravely wounded in battle. In 1809, he was promoted to Teniente General (Vice Admiral).

With the return of Fernando VII to the throne in 1814, Valdés was again out of favour. He was ordered to be confined to the fortress of Alicante, although the confinement was not as rigid as it sounds. He was allowed to exercise on horseback in the vicinity, as long as he stayed within the Governor's jurisdiction.

In 1817, the Cartagena squadron was in poor condition. Ships, equipment, and men had been allowed to deteriorate. Valdés was summoned from his confinement to inspect the fleet. He wrote his report from the fortress, where he returned after the inspection.

In 1820, when the constitution of 1812 was restored, Valdés was one of the liberals who returned to office. He was released, and appointed as both Civil and Military Governor of Cádiz, the base of the Atlantic fleet. The next year, at the age of fifty four, he married the Alicante widow who had petitioned for the retention of her pension if she married Valdés. He became a deputy in the Cortes in the same year, and was chosen as their President in 1822.

When Fernando was deposed in 1823, Valdés was one of the members of the Regency. The Cortes, or some of their members, moved to Cádiz, with Fernando as a virtual prisoner. In the end, Valdés had to hand the King back to the French, and fled to Gibraltar. He spent the next ten years in England, where any enemy of France was welcome.

With the amnesty to the liberals, Valdés was rehabilitated, and named Capitan General of Cádiz in 1835. In 1839, he died in Madrid at the age of seventy two.

JUAN VERNACCI Y RETAMAL was entered as a midshipman in 1780, which suggests that he was born about 1765. He was promoted to Alférez de Fragata two years later. Further promotion came slowly, and his father petitioned for his advancement from this rank five years later, citing the distinction of his family and their services to the State in various capacities.

At the end of 1794, Galiano asked for Vernacci's promotion from Frigate Lieutenant, the rank he then held, to Frigate Captain, a jump of two steps in rank. This was granted, but only on an acting basis, while he was working under Galiano in Madrid on the maps and documents of the voyage of *Sutil* and *Mexicana*.

Vernacci worked with Galiano until the latter stopped his work on the map of Spain in 1796, following which Vernacci joined the Naval Staff in Madrid as an "Agente Fiscal." He had reverted to his permanent rank as a lieutenant.

At some point, he returned to the Pacific, the only one of the officers of *Sutil* and *Mexicana* to do so, and in October 1802 he was in command of the "nao de Acapulco," another name for the Manila galleon. He also did some mapping in the Phillipines. By then, Vernacci had achieved the rank of Frigate Captain.

He died in Mexico on January 4, 1810, before the revolutionary movement had made itself felt.

SECUNDINO (DE) SALAMANCA Y HUMARA started his naval career as a midshipman in 1782. He progressed steadily, and was made a Frigate Lieutenant in 1789, while he was working on the preparations for the Malaspina voyage. He returned to Spain with Valdés in 1793, and became a Ship Lieutenant at that time. In 1795, his further promotion was requested by Galiano, along with Vernacci's. In Salamanca's case, the promotion stuck, and he was confirmed as a Frigate Captain in 1797. He finally achieved the rank of Brigadier in 1805.

Salamanca's name was dropped from the Navy List in 1811, apparently for political reasons, because by 1813 he was living in France as a refugee. Political matters settled down after Fernando had regained his throne in 1823, so Salamanca started petitioning for his rehabilitation. By 1826 he was able to return to Spain. His rank of Brigadier was restored, but not his pay, nor was there any employment for him. After writing more petitions, he was awarded half pay, but never served in the Navy again, dying in Madrid in 1839, by which time he would have been over seventy.

JOSÉ (OR JOSEF) CARDERO started out on the Malaspina voyage as a member of the crew of *Descubierta*, possibly as a servant. He had been born in 1766 in Ecija, not far from Galiano's birthplace in Córdoba province. Nothing is known of his life until he sailed with Malaspina at the age of twenty three. He showed an aptitude for drawing early in the voyage, but Malaspina did not mention this when he wrote a recommendation for Cardero in September 1790, and included his name on a list of crew members who deserved a good service bonus. One of the official artists left the expedition at Callao, where the ships were at that time, and Cardero made drawings regularly from then on.

When the ships reached Acapulco early in 1791, the other artist left, and Cardero's status as artist and map drawer was confirmed. As has been said in the Introduction, he was detached to join Galiano and Valdés in 1792 on the voyage of *Sutil* and *Mexicana*, unknowingly contributing the illustrations for this book. These illustrations show the naturalness of Cardero's work, and the limitations on his artistic ability. After the voyage, the painter Fernando Brambila, who had never seen the Northwest Coast, produced "improved" versions of Cardero's drawings in Madrid, which may have had more artistic merit, but were less accurate. In the Brambila copy of Cardero's drawing of the Canal de Salamanca, a baidar has been added. This is a skin boat used by the Aleuts, but unknown farther south.

Cardero's duties during the 1792 voyage included making fair copies of sketch maps as well as making drawings, and he was often included in the boat parties which were sent out to explore. Some of the manuscript maps are still in the Museo Naval, showing the neatness of hand characteristic of Cardero's work, even though the condition of some has deteriorated badly.

After the voyage, Cardero returned to Spain, and was with Valdés for a time. When Malaspina got back from the Pacific, Cardero turned over his drawings to him, but was informed in 1795 that his services were not needed on the work of putting all the documents and maps of the voyage in order.

He was immediately appointed as a Ship Accountant, or administrative official of the Navy, and sent to Cádiz. He seems to have done well, and his name was entered in the Navy List as a permanent officer in 1797. Apart from the appearance of his name annually in the Navy List, little is known of his life or work in those years. In 1811, his name disappeared from the List. Other names were removed for political reasons at that time, but the servant who became an artist, then an officer, might have died or resigned.

As far as is known, Cardero went on no more long voyages, nor was he ever again employed as an artist. He certainly would not have been employed as a servant.

GLOSSARY OF PLACE NAMES

Chapter	Spanish Name	Modern Name
XVIII	Alixos (Alijos), Islas	Rocas Alijos
XI	Aliponzoni, Ensenada	Some bay east of Frederick Arm
XI	Aliponzoni, Punta	Probably Horn Point
IX	Arco, Canal	Homfray Channel
IV	Arrecifes, Punta	Escalante Point
XIII	Atrevida, Canal	Queen Charlotte Strait
XII	Balda, Canal	S. part of Tribune Channel, plus Thompson Sound
XII	Baldinat, Canal	N. part of Tribune Channel
XII	Bauzá, Anclage	Probably Blenkinsop Bay
XII	Bernaci, Canal (Vernacci)	Knight Inlet
VI	Bonilla, Isla	Smith Island
XIV	Brooks, Puerto	Brooks Harbour
XIV	Bucareli, Puerto	Bucareli Bay
IV	Buena Esperanza, Boca	Esperanza Inlet
IX	Bustamante, Canal	Probably Theodosia Arm
V	Caamaño, Boca	Admiralty Inlet
XVIII	Californias, Peninsula	Baja California
XII	Canónigo, Brazo	Forward Harbour
X	Carbajal, Canal	Cordero Channel (part)
XII	Cárdenas, Anclage	Port Neville
X	Cardero, Canal	Cordero Channel (part)
VIII	Carmelo, Boca	Howe Sound
VI	Carmelo, Monte	Probably Mount Baker
X	Carvajal, Angostura	Cordero Channel (part)
XVIII	Catalina, Isla	See Santa Catalina
VI	Cepeda, Punta	Point Roberts
XVIII	Cerros, Golfo	The S. part is now Bahia de Sebastián Vizcaíno

XVIII	Cerros, Isla	Isla de Cedros
X	Cevallos, Isla	Stuart Island
IX	Comandantes, Angostura	Arran Rapids
XIV	Consolación, Cala	Probably west of Lemon Point
V	Córdova, Puerto	Esquimalt Harbour
XVIII	Coronados, Islas	Coronado Islands
XVIII	Cortes, Mar de	Gulf of California
VII	Descanso, Cala	Descanso Bay
XIII	Descubierta, Canal	Johnstone Strait
XIV	Deseado, Puerto (Argentina)	Port Deseado
XI	Engaño, Canal	Cordero Channel, (part)
XI	Estero, Ensenada	Frederick Arm
XII	Estrada, Ensenada	Exact location uncertain
XVI	Ezeta, Boca or Entrada	Mouth of Columbia River
XVI	Falcon, Cabo	Cape Falcon
XVI	Farallones de S. Francisco	Farallon Islands
V	Flon, Boca	Deception Pass
XII	Flores, Brazo	Topaze Harbour
V	Floridablanca, Canal	Non-existent
XIV	Frondoso, Cabo	Cape Cook
VI	Garzon, Ensenada	Birch Bay
VI	Gaston, Seno	Bellingham Bay
VII	Gaviola, Punta	Josef Pt., on Gabriola Island
XVI	Gorda, Punta	Brown Point
XIII	Gorostiza, Puerto	Shushartie Bay
VI	Güemes, Canal	Guemes Channel
VI	Güemes, Isla	Guemes Island
XIV	Güemes, Puerto	Hardy Bay
XII	Insulto, Anclage	At entrance of Havannah Channel
VII	Lángara, Punta	Point Grey
XIV	Lanz, Islas	Scott Islands
XVI	Lobos, Farallon	Probably Richardson Rock
VI	Loera, Ensenada	Lummi Bay
XVI	Maltiempo, Cabo	Cape Foulweather

XIV	Malvinas, Islas	Falkland or Malvinas Islands
XIV	Meir, Anclage	Close to Meir Point
XVI	Mendozino, Cabo	Cape Mendocino
XIV	Mexicana, Punta	Mexicana Point
VII	Moñino, Boca	Jervis Inlet
V	Moreno de la Vega, Punta	Race Rocks
VI	Morro, Islas	Allan and Burrows Islands
IV	Nitinat, Entrada	Barclay Sound
IV	Nitinat, Punta del E.	Cape Beale
X	Nodales, Canal	Nodales Channel
XIV	Norte, Cabo	Not identified
X	Novales, Anclage	Near Thynne Point
VI	Nuestra Señora del Rosario, Canal	Georgia Strait
VII	Nueva Holanda	Australia
XII	Nuevo Remolinos, Canal	Wellbore Channel
IV	Núñez Gaona	Neah Bay
X	Olavide, Canal	Cordero Channel, part
VII	Otaiti, Islas	Society Islands
VI	Pacheco, Canal	Hale Passage
IX	Pesquero, Bahía	Unnamed bay, E. of Zephine Head
XVIII	Pinos, Punta	Point Pinos
X	Pineda, Canal	Narrows at Irvine Point
VII	Porlier, Bocas	Porlier Pass
INSTR	Princesa Real, Isla	Princess Royal Island
V	Quadra, Puerto	Port Discovery
VIII	Quema, Isla	Kinghorn Island
V	Quimper, Bahía	Dungeness Harbor
IX	Quintano, Canal	Bute Inlet
IX	Remolinos, Canal	Yuculta Rapids
XII	Retamal, Canal	Call Inlet
XVI	Reyes, Punta	Point Reyes
INSTR	Reyna Carlota, Islas	Queen Charlotte Islands
XI	Salamanca, Canal	Loughborough Inlet
XIV	Salida de las Goletas	Goletas Channel

XVIII	San Andrés, Isla	San Clemente Island
XVI	San Cayetano	Possibly Chehalis Point
XVIII	San Diego, Puerto	San Diego Harbour
XVIII	San Diego, Punta	Point Loma
XIV	San José, Brazo	Quatsino Sound.
XVIII	San Lucas, Cabo	Cape San Lucas
XVIII	San Nicolas, Isla	San Nicolas Island
VI	San Rafael, Punta	Kwomais Point
XVI	San Roque, Cabo	Cape Disappointment
VII	Sandwich, Islas	Hawaiian Islands
XVIII	Santa Bárbara, Canal	Santa Barbara Channel
XVIII	Santa Catalina, Isla	Santa Catalina Island
IX	Sarmiento, Punta	Sarah Point
XIV	Scot, Cabo	Cape Scott
X	Separación, Canal	Lewis Channel
VI	Solano, Punta	William Point
XIV	Sutil, Punta	Sutil Point
IX	Tabla, Canal	Toba Inlet
XI	Tenet, Anclage	Location uncertain
VIII	Texada, Isla	Texada Island
XI	Torres, Canal	Clio Passage
VI	Tres Hermanas, Islas	Huckleberry and nearby islands
X	Tres Marías, Islas (Canada)	Rendezvous Islands
XVIII	Tres Marías, Islas (Mexico)	Islas Marías
XVIII	Trinidad, Isla (Mexico)	Isla Natividad
XIV	Valdés, Puerto	Bull Harbour
XII	Vernacci, Canal	Knight Inlet
XI	Viana, Anclage	Opposite Loughborough Inlet
XIV	Vilavicencio, Bahía	On south shore of Nigei Island
XI	Vueltas, Isla	Dent or Little Dent Island
VII	Winthuysen, Bocas	Nanaimo Harbour
XVIII	Ysabela, Isla (Mexico)	Isla Isabela

CORRESPONDENCE

Translator's note: The first item (Letter A) is an extract from a letter from Revillagigedo, the Viceroy of New Spain, to the Duke of Alcudia (better known under his original name of Manuel Godoy), the Minister of State in Madrid. It is taken from AHN Estado, Legajo 4289. The other three letters (B, C, and D) were exchanged between Revillagigedo and Galiano while the latter was in Veracruz waiting for a ship to Spain, They are found in Mexico in AGN Marina 92, and in Madrid in AHN Estado, Legajo 4289 and MN MS 280, f. 134 et seq.

A. Letter from Revillagigedo to Alcudia, 3 December, 1793.

Don Dionisio Alcalá Galiano and Ship Lieutenant Don Juan Bernaci (Vernacci) stayed in this capital for the purpose of correcting the chart and drawing up the diary, on which they started to work with their companions from the 11th of February of the present year, when they arrived in this capital.

Both [chart and diary] were delivered during the night of 18th October and on the 20th they left for Veracruz to embark in the ship San Pedro de Alcántara.

Having observed that in the diary there are some errors of the pen and defects of orthography, and that the maps or charts were missing the names of some of the places on the coasts which were explored, I thus advised him in the accompanying letter number 1, which at the same time makes clear that I know the worth of their hardships and anxieties, and offering to send to Your Excellency and to Señor Don Antonio Valdés[1] copies of the said documents with the corrections and additions appropriate to the end that they should bear all the perfection required by their importance.

At the very moment the mail was leaving for [Spain] I received the representation, of which I include a copy under number 2, in which Galiano and Bernaci ask me to send the original diary and maps to Sr. Valdés for examination by the Council of Generals[2] of the Navy.

---

[1] The Minister of the Navy.

[2] Naval officers of flag rank held the title of General; the use of the word Admiral as a rank came later.

I replied in the terms recorded in my letter, of which the attached copy is marked number 3, sending to Your Excellency the original documents because the commission which was the reason for their formation was initiated by the Ministry which is in your charge.

B. Letter from Revillagigedo to Galiano, 23 October, 1793.

No. 1

Two nights before the day you started your journey from this capital[3] to that port[4] you brought me the description and maps of the coasts explored by yourself and Frigate Captain Don Cayetano Valdés in the goletas Sutil and Mexicana from the 8th of March when you left Acapulco to the 23rd of the following November when they returned to San Blas. I have examined carefully and in detail these documents, which prove the worth of the hardships and anxieties with which they have been formed, showing with all possible accuracy the points on the part of the coast that could not be explored by the corvettes Descubierta and Atrevida in the year 91.

The same applies with respect to the discoveries in the Strait of Juan de Fuca carried out in the three months of navigation from the entry of the goletas in latitude 48 deg. 20 m. until your exit in 50 deg. 10 m., resulting from which [it is known] that Nootka is an island whose territory occupies the space of more than 60 leagues in length and in some places 20 leagues of width.

The description appears to me adequate for the clearest understanding of the two maps, but in it I have noted various errors of the pen and defects of orthography, and in the maps some place names have been forgotten or omitted, namely the Puntas de Moreno de la Vega, the Isla de Bonilla, Isla and Canal de Güemes, the Canal de Pacheco, the Bocas de Winthuysen, and the Puntas de San Rafael and Lángara.

In consequence, I have ordered the correction of the material defects of the description and the addition of the omitted points for [the purpose of] sending them to Their Excellencies the Ministers of State and of the Navy, with the perfection demanded by the importance and the use of these documents.

My comments on them affirm the care with which I have examined them, in proof of the appreciation which is deserved by documents which ought to be of the greatest importance and which I anticipate are worthy of The Royal pleasure of His Majesty and his Sovereign approval.

23rd of October, 1793.

---

[3] Mexico
[4] Veracruz

C. Letter from Galiano to Revillagigedo, 26 November, 1793

No. 2

With Don Juan Vernacci, I repeat to Your Excellency the due thanks for the honourable expressions in your letter of the 23rd of October immediately preceding, and for the good will with which you have excused the errors of the pen, the defects of orthography, and the quoted omission of names on the last map of the northwest part of the Estrecho de Fuca, which [seem] to us [to] have been very significant. We endeavoured to correct all those defects of orthography which might affect the true sense. For this reason, on delivering them I asked Your Excellency to excuse the errors so that we would be able to take advantage of the opportune time to take passage to Europe in the ship San Pedro de Alcántara in order to be employed in the actual circumstances called for by our just wishes.[5]

Considering now, in agreement with Vernacci, that the expedition of the goletas Sutil and Mexicana directed by Your Excellency can acquire a fitting lustre on examination by the Council of Generals of the work and maps with all the documents which have been produced, and which we have presented as was done with those of the Spanish Peninsula drawn up by Brigadier Don Vicente Tofiño, a particular satisfaction to all those who have taken part in [the expedition] following from the approval of such a respected tribunal, I appeal to the kindness and protection of Your Excellency and request of you to have them presented to His Excellency the Minister of the Navy, sending him the originals which we had the honour of delivering to you under the circumstance of our early departure for Europe, considering them to be more suitable than copies since these never achieve the degree of accuracy of their originals. I hope to be worthy of this grace on the part of Your Excellency in continuation of the kindness and protection towards the officers of the expedition of the goletas in which we have had the honour of serving under your orders.

May God grant you many years.

Veracruz, the 26th of November, 1793.

[Signed] Dionisio Alcalá-Galiano

---

[5] That is to say, participating in the work of preparing the Malaspina voyage publication, as indicated in Article 13 of Malaspina's instructions.

D. Letter from Revillagigedo to Galiano, 3rd December 1793.

No. 3

The repeated tokens that I have given of the worth and distinction which to me the expedition of Ship Captain Alejandro Malaspina has merited are absolutely unequivocal. [The same applies] to the officers assigned to it who have had the need to come to this capital during the stay of the corvettes in Acapulco. For this reason I arranged that the work you delivered to me at the time of your departure for that port, should be fair copied. I wish the documents to arrive before His Majesty with the greatest clarity through His Excellency the First Secretary of State. Nothing could truly be more in the interest of those officers who were engaged on the exploration of the Estrecho de Juan de Fuca in which you are included.

You are now asking me, in your letter of the 26th of the immediately past month in agreement with Ship Lieutenant Don Juan Bernaci that I should direct the originals to the general headquarters of the navy because copies can never achieve the degree of accuracy [of the originals]. I have no hesitation in repeating this proof of my desire to accommodate you, notwithstanding that you waited to make your request until the exact time that I was going to send the despatches of the Royal Service to Spain, but it must be understood that what is possible for me is to send the originals to the Duke of Alcudia who is the person with whom I must treat directly in this matter, and a copy of everything, after making the corrections set out in the attached list[6] to the Señor Bailío,[7] accompanied also by copies of my letter of 23rd of October and the letter in which you replied, in order that with everything in view His Excellency may make such disposition as he believes most suitable as far as examining them in the Council of Generals as you wish. It falls on me only to make it clear that for my part, I will have the greatest satisfaction if they shall be officially classed as well executed, exact, and worthy of appreciation.

May God grant you many years.

Mexico, 3rd of December, 1793.

---

[6] A list of errata, not translated or included here.

[7] A high rank in a military order. This refers to Antonio Valdés, the Naval Minister.

SHIP'S MANIFEST OF *SUTIL*

Translator's note: The manifest of *Mexicana* is similar to that of *Sutil*, and is listed only where there is a significant difference. In AGN Marina 82, there is a twenty page inventory of the rigging and equipment aboard *Sutil*, which has not been translated. The equivalent of various units of measurement are as follows:

The basic unit of length is the pie, equivalent to 0.278 metres, or eleven English inches. A pulgada is one twelfth of a pie, and a braza is six pies.

A tonelada is a unit of capacity of a ship's hold, obtained by applying a formula to the hull dimensions. It was later standardized as 2.83 cubic metres or 100 cubic feet.

The most frequently used measure of weight is the arroba, 11.5 kilograms, or approximately 25 English pounds. It was divided into 25 libras, and four arrobas made one quintal.

Another unit of weight is the marco. As a measure used for precious metals, it is 230 grams, about half an English pound, but this unit in the manifest may refer to some usual size of package.

The size of barrels other than the quarter and third ton casks is not known, nor is there any information on the pesos of tobacco or the various jugs and bottles.

Manifest showing the state in which H.M.'s schooner Sutil put to sea under the command of Frigate Captain Dionisio Alcalá Galiano.

CREW[1]

Function	No.
Commissioned officers	2
Soldier	1
Petty officers and tradesmen	3
Seaman gunners	7
Seamen	6
Total	19
Servant	1

Note: *Mexicana* had the same complement, plus the artist Cardero.

DIMENSIONS OF THE SHIPS.

	Pies	Pulgadas
Length (a)	50	3
Beam	13	3
Depth of hold	8	4
Keel length	46	10
Floor timbers	8	7
Draft at poop	6	2
Draft at prow	5	8
Toneladas	33	

(a) Length between perpendiculars in English shipbuilding terminology. It is the length on deck between the stem and the rudder post.

ANCHORS

	Weight	
No.	Arrobas	Libras
1	11	5
1	10	7
1	9	10

CABLES

1 of 7 (Pulgadas of circumference) and 120 (Brazas of length)
1 of 6 1/2 and 120

---

[1] The translations "commissioned officers" and "petty officers" in this table are approximate.

SAILS

	Sutil	Mexicana
Flying jib	1	1
Jib	2	2
Fore staysail	1	1
Topsail staysail	1	-
Fore topgallant sail	1	-
Fore topsail	2	1
Foresail	2	2
Main topgallant sail	1	-
Main topsail	2	1
Driver or spanker	2	2
Foresail studding sails	2	-
Fore topsail studding sails	2	-
Main topsail studding sails	2	-
Square sails	-	2[2]

ARMS AND AMMUNITION

18 muskets	3 pikes
24 pistols	5 lances
18 sabres	50 balls
3 axes	50 bags grapeshot
2 cutlasses	2 arrobas musket balls
4 arrobas 19 libras gunpowder	

FOOD

50 quintals of bread
16 quintals of evaporated soup[3]
The remainder sufficient for three and one half months.

WATER SUPPLY

6 quarter ton casks
19 one third ton casks
12 loading barrels
6 hand barrels
This comprises requirements for three and one half months.

ARTICLES FOR THE INDIANS

58 sheets of copper

---

[2] One of the square sails would be the square foresail used when running. The second was probably a spare, since there are spares for the other principal sails.

[3] Menestra. A mixture of vegetables with some meat, boiled down until almost solid.

18 axes
80 marcos of assortments of beads
2 marcos of ornaments
2 cases of hardware
4 quintals of nails

EXTRAS FOR THE WELFARE OF THE CREW

8 flasks of antiscorbutics
2 cases of paste for broth
3 jars of extracts (type not stated)
1 jug of syrup
2 barrels of spirits
2 barrels of vinegar
4 barrels of wine
25 arrobas (290 kg) of ham
100 heads of garlic
62 1/2 pesos of tobacco
9 jugs of oil
1 case of soap
Fishing tackle

ASTRONOMICAL AND PHYSICAL INSTRUMENTS

1 "Licot" pendulum
1 Dollon equatorial theodolite of 1 1/2 feet with heliometer
1 two foot achromatic telescope
1 chronometer, Arnold No. 344
2 thermometers
1 barometer
2 hand telescopes
2 sextants, the personal property of the officers

Translator's note. The equatorial theodolite is used for direct measurement of the declination and hour angle of a celestial body. The heliometer was used for measuring the angle between two celestial objects.

The pendulum was for measuring the acceleration of gravity. By carrying out this experiment in various latitudes, the ellipticity of the earth could be calculated. *Mexicana* carried similar instruments, but in addition, there were three artificial horizons and a eudiometer. The artificial horizons were containers holding a pool of mercury. If the actual horizon could not be seen, the angle between the sun or a star and its reflection in the mercury was measured and divided by two. The artificial horizons could only be used ashore. The eudiometer is an instrument which purported to measure the purity of the air.[4]

The manifest concludes with a formal statement which reads:

This ship left in seaworthy condition[5] equipped with spars on the basis of rigging as a brigantine and with select quality food. Under sail from the port of Acapulco the 8th of March, 1792.

[4] See note at the end of Chapter III.
[5] Literal translation "watertight."

BIBLIOGRAPHY

Anon. 1802. *Relación del Viage hecho por . . . Sutil y Mexicana . . . 1792*. Madrid. Republished 1958. Cited as *"Viage."*

Archivo General de la Nación, Mexico. Various references. Cited as "AGN."

Archivo Histórico Nacional, Madrid. Various references. Cited as "AHN."

Barwick, G.F., 1911. (Translator). *Voyage of Sutil and Mexicana in 1792*. Unpublished typescript. Vancouver Public Library. See Anon., *Viage*.

Beaglehole, J.C., 1967. *The voyage of* Resolution *and* Discovery *: Introduction*. Hakluyt Society.

Beals, Herbert K., 1985. (Translator). *For Honor and Country: The Diary of Bruno de Hezeta*. Oregon Historical Society Press.

Bodega y Quadra, Juan Francisco de la, 1792. *Viage a la Costa . . . Septentrional*. MS in Archivo, Ministerio de Asuntos Exteriores, Madrid.

Burriel, Andrés Marcos, 1757. See Venegas.

Cerezo Martínez, Ricardo, 1987. *La Expedición Malaspina, Tomo I*. Museo Naval, Madrid.

Enciclopedia General del Mar. Madrid.

Higueras Rodriguez, Dolores, 1987. *Catálogo Crítico de los Documentos de la Expedición Malaspina*. Madrid, Museo Naval.

Jane, Cecil, 1930. (Translator). *A Spanish Voyage to Vancouver* (sic) *and the Northwest Coast of America*. Argonaut. See Anon., *Viage*.

Kendrick, John, 1985. *The Men with Wooden Feet: The Spanish Exploration of the Pacific Northwest*. NC Press, Toronto.

Lamb, W. Kaye, 1984. (Editor). *The Voyage of George Vancouver*. Hakluyt Society.

Moziño, José Mariano, 1792. *Noticias de Nutka*. Published 1913, Mexico.

Museo Naval, Madrid. Various references. Cited as "MN."

Novo y Colson, Pedro, 1885. (Editor). *Viage . . . de las Corbetas* Descubierta *y* Atrevida. Madrid.

Petrie, Charles, 1971. *King Charles III of Spain*. Constable, London.

Salvá, Jaime, n.d. (?ca. 1950). *Alcalá Galiano*. Madrid.

Sotos Serrano, Carmen, 1982. *Pintores de la Expedición Malaspina*. Real Academia de Historia, Madrid.

Stewart, Hilary, 1984. *Cedar*. Douglas and McIntyre, Vancouver.

Venegas, Miguel, 1757. *Noticia de California*. Attributed by Beaglehole (q.v.) to Andrés Marcos Burriel.

Wagner, H.R., 1933. *Spanish Explorations of the Strait of Juan de Fuca*. Fine Arts Press.

————, 1937. *Cartography of the Northwest Coast of America to the year 1800*. University of California Press.

Wilson Engstrand, I.H., 1970. (Translator). *Noticias de Nutka*. McLelland and Stewart. (See Moziño).

INDEX

The index covers the Introduction, the Voyage Instructions, the Dramatis Personae, and the Appendixes as well as the main text. Entries in the Bibliography are not included in the index, nor are modern toponyms for places on the Northwest Coast named by the Spanish. These are to be found in the Glossary of Place Names.